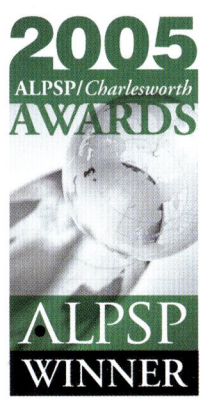

Textile

EDITED BY
PENNINA BARNETT
AND DORAN ROSS

THE JOURNAL OF
CLOTH AND CULTURE

VOLUME 3
ISSUE 3
FALL 2005

ORDERING INFORMATION
Three Issues per volume. One volume per annum, 2005: Volume 3

ONLINE
www.bergpublishers.com

BY MAIL
Berg Publishers
C/O Extenza-Turpin Distribution (Customer Services Dept)
Pegasus Drive
Stratton Business Park
Biggleswade
Bedfordshire SG18 8TQ
UK

BY FAX
+ 44 (0)1767 601640

BY TELEPHONE
+ 44 (0)1767 604800

For Enquiries
email subscriptions@turpinltd.com

ENQUIRIES
Editorial: Kathryn Earle, Managing Editor,
email kearle@bergpublishers.com

Production: Ken Bruce,
email kbruce@bergpublishers.com

Advertising: Veruschka Selbach,
email vselbach@bergpublishers.com

SUBSCRIPTION DETAILS
Free Online Subscription for Print Subscribers

Full color images available online.

Access your electronic subscription through
www.ingentaconnect.com

Institutional base list subscription price:
US$205.00, £115.00

Individuals' subscription price: US$78.00, £45.00

Berg Publishers is the imprint of
Oxford International Publishers Ltd.

EDITORS
Pennina Barnett
Goldsmiths College, UK

Doran Ross
UCLA Fowler Museum of Cultural History

Associate Editor
Mary Littrell, Colorado State University
mlittrel@cah.colostate.edu

Editorial Assistant
Janet Gilburt
rooster.gilburt@virgin.net

Book Reviews Editor:
Please send all books for consideration for review in Textile to:
Victoria Mitchell
Norwich School of Art & Design, St George Street, Norwich
NR3 1BB, UK
v.mitchell@nsad.ac.uk

Exhibition Reviews Editors:
UK and Rest of World
Jennifer Harris, The Whitworth Art Gallery, University of Manchester, Whitworth Park, Manchester M15 6ER, UK
jennifer.harris@man.ac.uk

USA
Rebecca Stevens, Contemporary Textiles, The Textile Museum, 23250 S Street NW, Washington, DC 20008-4088, USA
stevensgrj@aol.com

AIMS AND SCOPE
Cloth accesses an astonishingly broad range of human experiences. The raw material from which things are made, it has various associations: sensual, somatic, decorative, functional and ritual. Yet although textiles are part of our everyday lives, their very familiarity and accessibility belie a complex set of histories, and invite a range of speculations about their personal, social and cultural meanings. This ability to move within and reference multiple sites gives textiles their potency.

This journal brings together research in textiles in an innovative and distinctive academic forum for all those who share a multifaceted view of textiles within an expanded feld. Representing a dynamic and wide-ranging set of critical practices, it provides a platform for points of departure between art and craft; gender and identity; cloth, body and architecture; labor and technology; techno-design and practice—all situated within the broader contexts of material and visual culture.

Textile invites submissions informed by technology and visual media, history and cultural theory; anthropology; philosophy; political economy and psychoanalysis. It draws on a range of artistic practices, studio and digital work, manufacture and object production.

SUBMISSIONS
Should you have a topic you would like us to consider, please send an abstract of 300–500 words to one of the editors. Notes for Contributors can be found at the back of the journal and style guidelines are available by emailing kbruce@bergpublishers.com or from the Berg website (www.bergpublishers.com).

© 2005 Berg. All rights reserved. No part of this publication may be reproduced or utilized in any form or by any means, electronic or mechanical, including photocopying and recording, or by any information storage or retrieval system, without permission in writing from the publisher.

ISSN: 1475-9756
www.bergpublishers.com

INTERNATIONAL ADVISORY BOARD

Ingrid Bachmann
Concordia University, Canada

Elizabeth Barber
Occidental College, USA

Dilys Blum
Philadelphia Museum of Art, USA

Grace Cochrane
Powerhouse Museum, Australia

Susan Conway
Parson's School of Design, USA, and the British Museum, UK

Jasleen Dhamija
Independent Scholar/Consultant, India

Ian Hunter
Manchester Metropolitan University, UK

Janis Jefferies
Goldsmiths College, UK

Sarat Maharaj
Goldsmiths College, University of London, UK

Claire Pajaczkowska
Middlesex University, UK

John Picton
School of Oriental and African Studies, University of London, UK

Mary Schoeser
Freelance Historian, USA and UK

Lotus Stack
Minneapolis Institute of the Arts, USA

Nick Stanley
Birmingham Institute of Art and Design, UK

Anne Wilson
The School of the Art Institute of Chicago, USA

Diana Wood Conroy
University of Wollongong, Australia

On Stuff and Nonsense: The Complexity of Cloth
Claire Pajaczkowska

T-shirts, Testimony and Truth: Memories of Violence made Visible
Kimberly Miller

Inside out, Outside in: Unfolding a Territory of Process, Material and Meaning
Gerard Williams and Sally O'Reilly

Resistance and Submission, Warp and Weft: Unraveling the Life of Ethel Mairet
Kirsty Robertson

Exhibition Review
The *arttextiles* Project: An Ongoing Concern
Reviewed by Polly Binns

Contents

EDITORS
Pennina Barnett
Department of Visual Arts
Goldsmiths College
University of London
New Cross
London SE14 6NW
UK
p.barnett@gold.ac.uk

Doran Ross
UCLA
Fowler Museum of Cultural History
308 Charles Young Drive
Los Angeles, CA 90095-1549
USA
dross@arts.ucla.edu

TEXTILE HISTORY

Textile History is an internationally recognized, peer reviewed journal and one of the leading publications in its field. It is viewed as an important outlet for current research. Published in the spring and autumn of each year, its remit has always been to facilitate the publication of high-quality research and discussion in all aspects of scholarship arising from the history of textiles and dress.

The journal is now abstracted and indexed in *America: History and Life, Art and Archaeology Technical Abstracts, Arts and Humanities Citation Index, Art Index, Artbibliographies Modern, Avery Index to Architectural Periodicals, British and Irish Archaeological Bibliography, British Humanities Index, Current Contents/Arts & Humanities, Geographical Abstracts, Historical Abstracts, Textile Technology Digest, World Textile Abstracts* and *World Textiles*.

TEXTILE HISTORY RE-LAUNCHED FOR 2005!

The re-launch of *Textile History* includes a new design – both on the cover and internally – and the inclusion of full-colour illustration throughout which will enhance the text considerably and is a crucial feature of scholarship in this area.

NOW AVAILABLE ONLINE!

The full text of *Textile History* (together with tables of contents and abstracts) is now available online via IngentaConnect at
www.ingentaconnect.com/content/maney/tex

View a FREE SAMPLE ISSUE at:
www.ingentaconnect.com/content/maney/tex

CALL FOR PAPERS

To view the full Notes for Contributors please visit:
www.maney.co.uk/journals/notes/textile

EDITORS
Beverly Lemire
Department of History and Classics, University of Alberta, Canada

Lesley Miller
University of Southampton, UK

SUBSCRIPTION INFORMATION
Volume 36 (2005), 2 issues per year
Print ISSN: 0040-4969
Online ISSN: 1743-2952
Individual rate: £24.00/US$45.00
Institutional rate (including online access): £68.00/US$126.00

For further information please contact:
Maney Publishing, UK. Tel: +44 (0)113 249 7481 Fax: +44 (0)113 248 6983
Email: subscriptions@maney.co.uk
Or
Maney Publishing North America. Tel (toll free): 866 297 5154 Fax: 617 354 6875
Email: maney@maneyusa.com

For further information or to subscribe online please visit:
www.maney.co.uk

CALL FOR PAPERS

Textile Special Issue on STRING

Textile: The Journal of Cloth and Culture is proposing a special issue on "String," to be edited by Pennina Barnett (Goldsmiths, University of London) and Claire Pajaczkowska (Middlesex University). The topic can be interpreted literally, metaphorically or conceptually.

If you would like to submit a paper, or know of some interesting work on this theme, please send either an abstract of 500 words or a first draft to the editors before 1 May 2006. Contact emails: Pennina Barnett at p.barnett@gold.ac.uk and Claire Pajaczkowska at c.pajaczkowska@mdx.ac.uk

---

CALL FOR PAPERS

Textile Special Issue on SHAPING SPACE: TEXTILES AS ARCHITECTURE AND ARCHAEOLOGY

Textile: The Journal of Cloth and Culture is proposing a special issue on "Shaping Space: Textiles as Architecture and Archaeology," to be edited by Professor Janis Jefferies (Goldsmiths College, University of London) and Dr. Diana Wood Conroy (University of Wollongong).

This special issue seeks to commission and invite essays that explore contemporary textile theory with substantial historical scholarship in relation to issues raised by textiles as architecture. This might be in an archaeological context defining ideas of place, space and measurement through myth and narrative or though the use of textiles by architects for acoustic purposes. We are also interested in contributions that address how sustainable textile building technologies are being applied in contemporary architecture through the use of new materials and methods of fabrication in electronic architecture.

If you would like to submit a paper, please send a first draft to the editors by 1 January 2006. Contact emails: j.jefferies@gold.ac.uk and dconroy@uow.edu.au

Advised deadlines

1st draft submissions: 1 January 2006
2nd submissions: 1 February 2006
Peer-review process: 1 March 2006
Final submissions: 1 May 2006

On Stuff and Nonsense:
The Complexity of Cloth

Harriet B. Plimpton
Died Aug. 17, 1871.
Æ. 47 yrs. 9 ms.

Abstract

In the spectrum of losses that structures life from birth to death, the presence of cloth is a central signifier that differentiates nature from culture. Cloth thereby remains forever liminal in its cultural significance. This liminality is held, like a smell, in the meaning of the word "stuff," a translation of the French étoffe or cloth. Stuff has become, colloquially, a term used to designate generic "thingness," or unspecified materiality, in a way that gives eloquent expression to our culture's ambivalent relationship to textiles and to the tactile. We experience cloth as neither object nor subject, but as the threshold between, as a liminality where meaning decomposes into materiality, and threatens nonsense. It is this quality of non-sense that makes textiles especially interesting.

CLAIRE PAJACZKOWSKA

Claire Pajaczkowska is Reader in Psychoanalysis and Visual Culture in the School of Arts, Middlesex University. This paper was written as part of the research on the sublime made possible by the Leverhulme Foundation's Research Fellowship, conducted between 2002–2004. The generosity of the Leverhulme Foundation and Middlesex University's Research funding is, here, gratefully acknowledged. Other papers from this research include "Urban memory/suburban oblivion" in *Urban Memory*, Mark Crinson, ed: Routledge, 2005; "Perversion in French avant garde art 1912–1916" in *Perversion*, Lisa Downing and Dany Nobus, eds: Karnac, 2005; and "The Garden of Eden: sex, shame and knowledge" in *Shame and Sexuality*, Claire Pajaczkowska and Adrian Rifkin, eds: Freud Museum, 2006. A book on the sublime is forthcoming.

On Stuff and Nonsense: The Complexity of Cloth

The appearance of a new journal *Textile: The Journal of Cloth and Culture* in 2003, marked a significant moment in the discourse of visual culture, the nature of which is explored here. Despite the fact that the cultural significance of textiles extends well beyond visual culture, so that the journal *Textile* publishes research from anthropology and social history as well as art and design, the fact that it has emerged from the Visual Arts Department of Goldsmiths' College, University of London, offers an important dimension in the complex and multi-disciplinary significance of textiles in culture. The new thinking on textiles enables the conceptualization of the "visual" to be re-framed and reconsidered in ways that extend the existing discourse of cultural theory and art into an area that is more challenging and more generative, yielding problems of depth and complexity.

That the new journal brings together the disparate discourses within which the study of textiles has, over the past decades, been disseminated is, in itself, one of the reasons for its importance: initiating a pioneering moment in establishing the parameters and terms of a new discursive practice. A new cultural and intellectual autonomy has been won for textiles, through the intellectual creativity that is characteristic of the innovative tradition of the British school of art. This intellectual ethos is one that can comprehend many opposing forces within and outside the corpus of textile theory—the tensions between the opposing and disparate elements of avant garde and industrial practices, individual and social practices, the craft and the conceptual dimensions, the handmade, the manufactured and the computer-generated, the tactile and the visual, intellectual, corporeal and affective practices. To these antitheses we will add further contradictions that can be found in the warp and weft of cloth, in its frayed edges, in its twin functions of hiding and revealing, protecting and shrouding that are implicit in the cultural significance of cloth. The juxtaposition of contradictory and antithetical elements within the discourse of textiles revolves, ultimately, around the fulcrum of the founding contradiction of cloth—its double status—like the recto and verso of a sheet of paper which is a metaphor for the implication of the unconscious in the real, between the reality of cloth as material and cloth as symbol. That materiality always signifies, and that signification is always, also, material is the dimension of the contradiction of textiles that we shall explore.

This journal enables the new conceptualization of textiles as a component of culture generating its own object and terms of inquiry, its own methods of scholarship, research and knowledge. Textiles have, over the last decade, emerged as a distinct cultural practice as well as being conceptualized as a specific social and textual practice within culture conceived more generally. In her editorial, Pennina Barnett explores these new directions in the study of textiles, discussing some linguistic metaphors, as powerful as they are ubiquitous, that the experience of textiles offers to the lexicon we use to form our everyday conceptualization of reality. Are textile metaphors to be explained or to be enjoyed? *Ex-planere*, to explain, is derived from the Latin, "to unfold," similarly, in French, *expliquer* is derived from *explier*. Through the perspective offered by this new discourse on cloth and culture we are made conscious of the significance of the metaphors of folding and unfolding, the "folds of memory" as vivid imagery of the enigma of the seen and the unseen in consciousness and forgetting. We intuit the meanings of enveloping, draping, covering and clothing as gestures of touching, possessing and protecting (Doy 2002). We intuit the significance of wrapping as a prosthesis of touch, the continued existence of the hand in the absence of the body that offers touch. We intuit the imbrication and interplay between touch and sight. We sense the antithetical dynamic between hiding and revealing, concealment and exhibition. With Barnett we note Gilles Deleuze's conception of the fold as metaphor of Baroque epistemology."[1] Through and beyond Deleuze, we can explore the pliabilities of the textile metaphor, through the etymological roots of the pli that generates the implication, complication, multiplications and perplexity, among other associated concepts, propose that the new interface of cloth and culture, celebrated and to some extent created by the new journal, offer a radical departure for rethinking the complexities of representation and the body. Philosophy, such as Deleuze's, may take us some way into the exploration but other discourses offer tools for deconstructing the meanings of the bodily and corporeal such as its sensibilities, its sexuality, its unconscious, its gendered and its infantile dimensions. That the textile arts, more than any other, implicate the body as corporeal reality is the thesis explored here. The means for exploring this include observation of textiles in use and in their representation as symbol, and through the interpretation of such observation, using psychoanalysis and its concepts.

Anne Hamlyn's paper in the same, first, issue of *Textile*, "Freud, Fabric, Fetishism" proposes a double critique of Freud and of the psychoanalytic concept of fetishism, while demonstrating the challenge offered by psychoanalytic perspectives on textiles, such as the unspoken significance of touch and sensual, embodied meaning. Here I pick up the "thread" of Hamlyn's thought, elaborating the concept of the fetishism of textiles, and relating this also to the status of cloth as "uncanny." Both Barnett's and Hamlyn's papers indicate a new potential for explaining (or unfolding) the deeply enigmatic and obscure relation between the area of experience that has been named, in Kristevan terms, the "pre Symbolic," (Kristeva 1974, 1980) and the meaning of fabric as related to tactility and the sense of touch, what Barnett encompasses within the "haptic:" relation between tactile, visual, embodied and Symbolic registers of meaning which exists at the center of the subjective experience of culture. When Barnett (1999) proposed a new analytic idiom for describing culture based on a form that is less "box thought" and more informed by the Deleuzian "fold" and by Michel Serres,[2] she offers a coherent post-Enlightenment project through which we may reach through to the depths of meaning that Euclidean, mathematical and rationalist, geometry and its vestigial remains in discourses of mastery tried, so actively, to avoid. Barnett's comparison between the rigid and geometrical paradigms of empirical science and the "soft logic" of post-structuralist thought is a metaphor for the topographies of visibility and opacity, tactility and embodiment in contemporary thought.

I propose that psychoanalysis has an important part to play in this new understanding of embodied thought that the new discourse on textiles offers as its most fundamental challenge. The concept of fetishism is indispensable in conceptualizing both cloth and culture, and fetishism can usefully be understood as one end of a psychic spectrum that spans to the sublime. The extremes of objectification and engulfment feature insistently and repeatedly in our experience and understanding of textiles. Anne Hamlyn's paper proposes a critique of Freud's concept of fetishism while finding use for some kind of understanding of the particular fascination that fabrics can have, holding spectators in a fantasy that has no rational explanation. If we understand the liminality of textiles, its "stuff" and its nonsense, we find a curious interplay between maternal and phallic, between distance and proximity, between sight and touch and between sacred and profane.

Starting from philosophy, then, the Deleuzian hypothesis is that the fold characterizes Baroque thought, it engulfs and envelops, defying the Euclidean perspectives of the Renaissance and its monocular subjectivity, the fold embodies a perspective from which God is always omnipresent.[3] For us, however, it is more important that in the fold there are surfaces and planes which are known to exist but which are not accessible to view. The fold is a plane that curves back on itself in a recursive and reflexive way, knowledge of which defies not only the Euclidean perspective but also rationalist and empirical logic. Martin Jay proposed the concept of a Baroque scopic regime, distinct from Renaissance geometry, which embodies the curvilinear surface (Jay 1997). The fold has an underside that defines it as much as its visible surface. The Deleuzian project now (Deleuze 2001; Rachman 2001; Robinson 2001), consciously or not, recapitulates a Kristevan challenge to the tyrannical "dream of symmetry" that has dominated science and philosophy ever since the eighteenth century. This is one reason why his writing is of interest to those rethinking the cultural representation of sex and gender.

When reflecting on the affective spectrum that unites the Baroque sublime and the fetishistic it is psychoanalysis that offers a means of exploring the hidden, the unseen, what lies beneath and "forgotten" or implicit, and is an essential component of the theory of cloth and culture. Whether analysis is a form of mastery and control, or a form of knowledge and liberation depends on how it is used, and by whom. Here, I explore some ways of considering the realities of unconscious fantasy, emotional reality, embodied knowledge. I explore the concept of the Symbolic order as a fantasy of static omniscience, and as the Law, that is based on a repression of bodily movement, subjective perspective. This challenge to the rationalist fantasy of Enlightenment perspective and what Barnett nominates as "ocularcentrism," is based on a psychoanalytic understanding of culture as a product of the unconscious. The unconscious defined by psychoanalysis and refined by newer developments in brain science and neuro-anatomy, comprises series of reflexes and automatic behaviors that are not always adaptable to conscious will. Before the evolution of the bipedal gait and upright posture, the sense of sight was not so central in the organization of the brain. Attachment was regulated by touch and sexuality by smell.

The Moro reflex in newborn infants, which enables a baby to grip tight is a vestigial remnant of this pre-ocularcentric subjectivity, and the senses of touch and tactility retain very significant meaning in the contemporary experience of attachment and relationship. This has further been analyzed by Winnicott (1957), observing babies' use of blanket, cloth or soft cloth toy: the textile is important as it retains smell which is central to the significance of the object for the infant, it enables the infant to make the transition from narcissistic to object relationships. Winnicott further analyzes this game of transitional object as a precursor to the place of culture as transitional space. We shall return to this exploration of the centrality of the tactile, or what Pennina Barnett refers to as the "haptic," at several times in order to account for the strangely eccentric, uncannily central significance of cloth in our culture. Recent studies on the cultural significance of skin explore this relationship between the textual and the tactile (Benthian 2002).

Another way of deconstructing the centrality of vision in our culture is to understand the gaze as an unconscious or infantile

Figure 1
Pennants and pennons—naval and military flags. *I See All, Picture Encyclopaedia* Vol. 4: Arthur Mee, London c.1924.

Figure 2
Cushions. *I See All, Picture Encyclopaedia* Vol. 2: Arthur Mee, London 1934.

gaze, rather than the disembodied omniscience of the Enlightenment "eye of God" or the seventeenth-century Cartesian Cogito. The gaze, understood as infantile and unconscious, implies a different kind of subject and a different relationship of the subject to the rational.

The psychoanalytic view of culture sees culture as a representational world which shows the material embodiment of the human need for the double movement that recapitulates the "before" of infancy and the unconscious, within a movement "beyond," and onward towards the sublime, the need to transcend limits or transgress boundaries. The need to *depasser les limites* which, as Janine Chasseguet-Smirgel (1989) has noted, co-exists as the original matrix of pre-Symbolic subjectivity and as the origin of cultural creativity.

The existence of this interaction of tactile, visual and Symbolic registers as material reality is obscured by the fact that this dynamic is experienced as unconscious and therefore

Figure 3
Damask—ancient and modern examples of figured fabrics. *I See All, Picture Encyclopaedia* Vol. 2: Arthur Mee, London, 1934.

emotional or bodily reality. This associative chain through which meaning is begotten from the body is one of the possible interpretations offered by psychoanalysis. Another interpretation, centering on the libidinal and Oedipal structures that Freud described as the "nuclear complex" of the mind and of culture interprets the unconscious as a nuclear reactor of fusion and fission which generates and binds enough energy to fuel or fire the representational world. The orbit of electrons around a nucleus, atoms combining in molecular compounds offers a metaphor of culture that is dynamic and not static, as are the models proposed by social scientists. The Freudian metaphor of libido, from *libere*, "to pour," (an etymological root which also gives us liberation) has the limitations of the hydraulic images of nineteenth-century mechanistic science. However it understands culture as a representational world in which "unbound energy" motivates the "binding" of the Symbolic order. Whether conceived as the "nuclear" complex or as society's consolation for giving up the satisfaction and pleasures of infantile omnipotence, this relationship lies at the interface between the primary processes of metaphor and metonymy, and the secondary processes of syntactic language. It is good to remember then, the etymology of "analysis," from the Latin *ana-liese* (*lier* in French, means "to tie or link"), which simply means "to loosen the ties" (Panofsky 1964).

An example may illustrate the psychoanalytic concept of the relationship between an unseen infantile experience and the representational world of culture. Considering Piero Della

Francesca's Madonna del Parto we realize that representations of pregnancy are not common within the western tradition of art, and since the paradox of sexuality and generation lies at the core of the unconscious Oedipal complex, the representation of the Madonna as pregnant is depicted through a visual language of the interplay of seen and unseen, of what is known and what is not-known. The interplay of seen and hidden, is, in the painting, represented as what is draped and what is undraped. Cloth is the medium depicted for representing the contradictory reality of motherhood as both sexual and protective, as this contradiction exists for the community of spectators for whom this Madonna is either a work of beauty or meaning. The Madonna points to the opening in her clothes, an aperture that is as shocking as any violation of boundary in the social corpus through excess or vulnerability, indicating the fecundity of the maternal body that holds the unborn Christ, a gesture that is replicated in the posture of the two angels at either side who hold back the curtain which marks the proscenium arch of figurative art. The formal motif of uncovering and undraping to reveal the body of the painting and the body of the mother shows us the parallel between the infantile experience of corporeal reality and the unconscious meaning of the representational world of imagery. The content, if you like, is Oedipal, whereas the form is pre-Oedipal, and each replicates the other in a visual game of rhyming, repetition and echo. The visual equivalent of echo is mirroring, although the replication in this image is not one of identity but of difference. What is unveiled by the angels is a scene of maternal nurturing and protection, while what is being unveiled at the mother's abdomen is the hidden origins of unborn man. The curtain that has been opened, by our gaze, and the helpful angels, messengers of God, the word, is an iconic representation of the enigma of unconsciousness or what is hidden from us by the "curtain" of repression.

That the spectators gaze is first and foremost an infantile gaze is a proposition to be explored in greater depth. That the gaze is mediated by curtains as symbols of the unseen and unseeable is also of primary significance.

The textile materiality of the medium of knowing and not knowing is significant. Rather than demonstrating the antithesis between the seen and the unseen through, for example, light and dark which isolates the visual as the metaphor for consciousness, this textile metaphor implicates the tactile. The corporeal and infantile meanings of touch, and specifically touch as creation of the maternal body, are structured into the visual interplay of both form and content of this painting.

We find similar uses of the medium of cloth, funereal shrouds, veiled urns and the drapery that is commonly found carved in stone on tombstone architecture (see Panofsky 1964). Freud's essay on "Mourning and Melancholia" gives ample evidence of the significance of the psychic interplay of loss and refinding as the elementary structure of mourning. The thoughts in his "Beyond the Pleasure Principle" extend this concept of the centrality of loss to the formation of a representational object, into a theory of the structuration of absence within the phonemics and syntax of representation itself. In the spectrum of losses that structure life from birth to death the presence of cloth is a central signifier that differentiates nature from culture, and thereby remains forever liminal in its cultural significance. This liminality is held, like a smell in the meaning of the word "stuff," a translation of the French word *étoffe*, cloth. It has become a term for generic "thingness," unspecified materiality, in way that eloquently represents our ambiguous relationship to textiles that we experience as neither object nor subject, but as the threshold between. It is this quality of non-sense that makes textiles especially interesting.

Figure 4
Tombstone with bible and curtain, 1871, Oak Ridge Cemetery, MA, USA.

Figure 5
Tombstone with bible and curtain, 1871, Oak Ridge Cemetery, MA, USA.

Fusion, Paradox and Recursivity

Textile as a word is derived from the same root as *tisser*, "to spin and to weave;" *un tissu* in French, is a cloth or woven cloth. The confusion, in English, as to whether the word "textiles" ought to be used as a singular or plural noun remains as much a matter of usage as of grammatical correctness. Moreover, and to add another fold to the recursivity of language, our students conceive of, or describe, themselves as "doing" textiles, which adds the confusion over whether this singular or plural noun is also a verb. I suspect that these generic and grammatical confusions reflect the profound paradox, the fission and fusion between subject and object, at the nuclear core of textiles. For example, activity and passivity of being clothed expresses the same antithetical meaning that Freud noted in such ancient verbs as "to cleave," meaning to divide and to cling, as well as adjectives such as "alter" meaning both high and deep (Freud 1911). As Hamlyn notes in her paper, to touch is always also to be touched. This paradoxical, recursive logic that confounds the

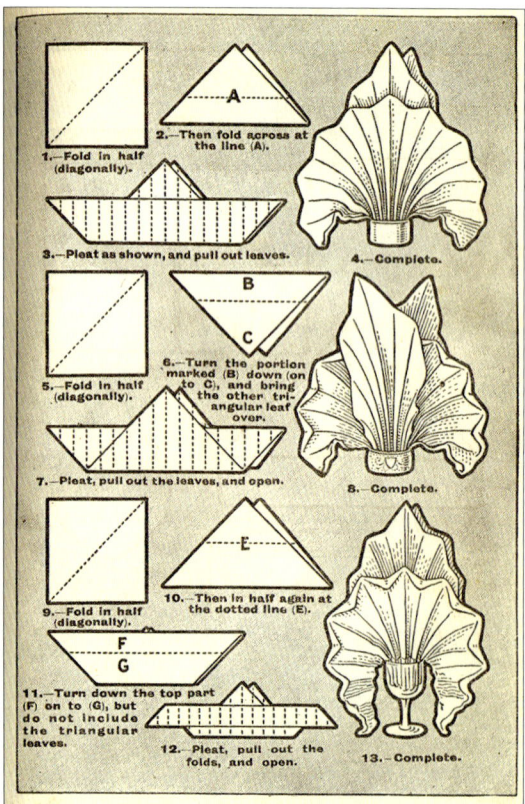
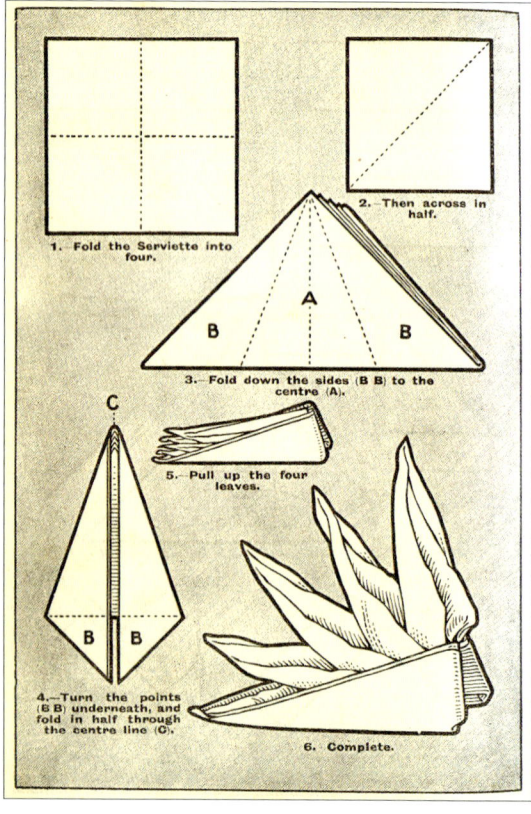

Figure 6
Table napkins—(A) The fleur de lys; (B) The cockscomb. *Mrs Beeton's Book of Household Management*, London, 1921.

Figure 7
Nursing 2. *Mrs Beeton's Book of Household Management*, London, 1921.

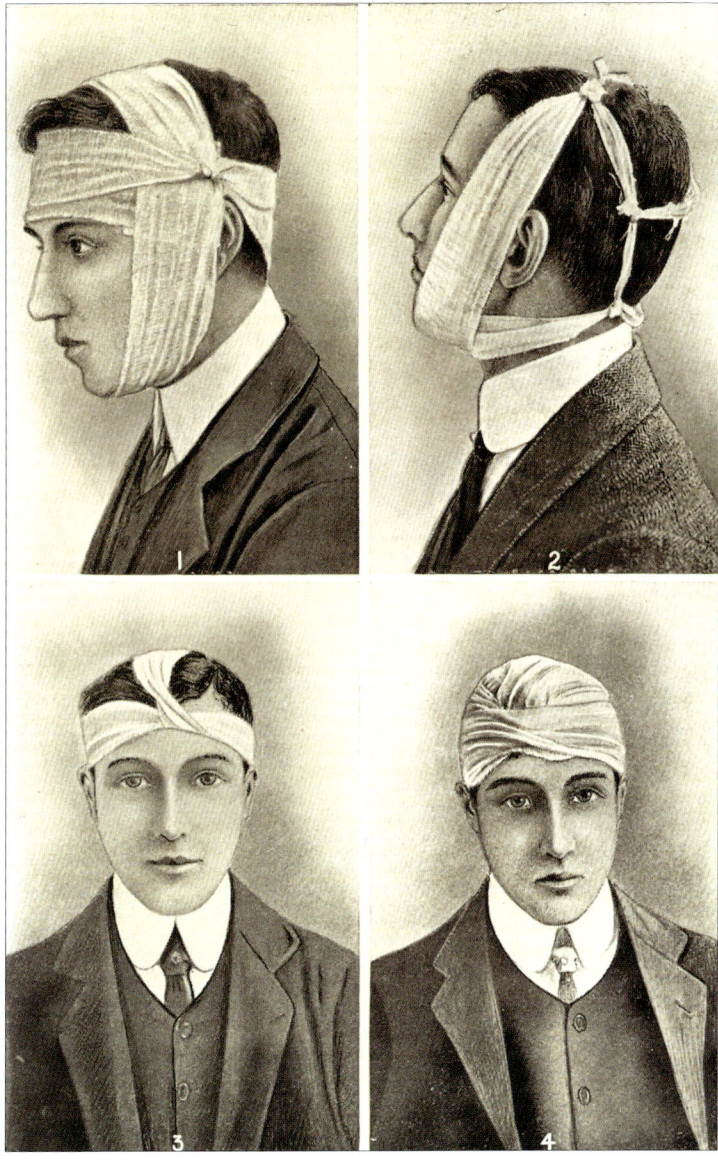

logic of syntactic Symbolic order, the law of grammatical correctness, is the voice of what Kristeva calls the "semiotic," what Irigaray nominates as the "feminine," and what Chasseguet-Smirgel calls the pre-Oedipal.[4] The impossibility of putting into words the knowledge and experience expressed by these antitheses is the dynamic that gives the most profound significance to the cultural status of textiles. There is, contained in the paradoxical and therefore anxiogenic meanings of cloth in our culture, a manifestation of the deepest, most primitive mammalian drive to make a place, to protect and house, to meet the needs of the first human relation

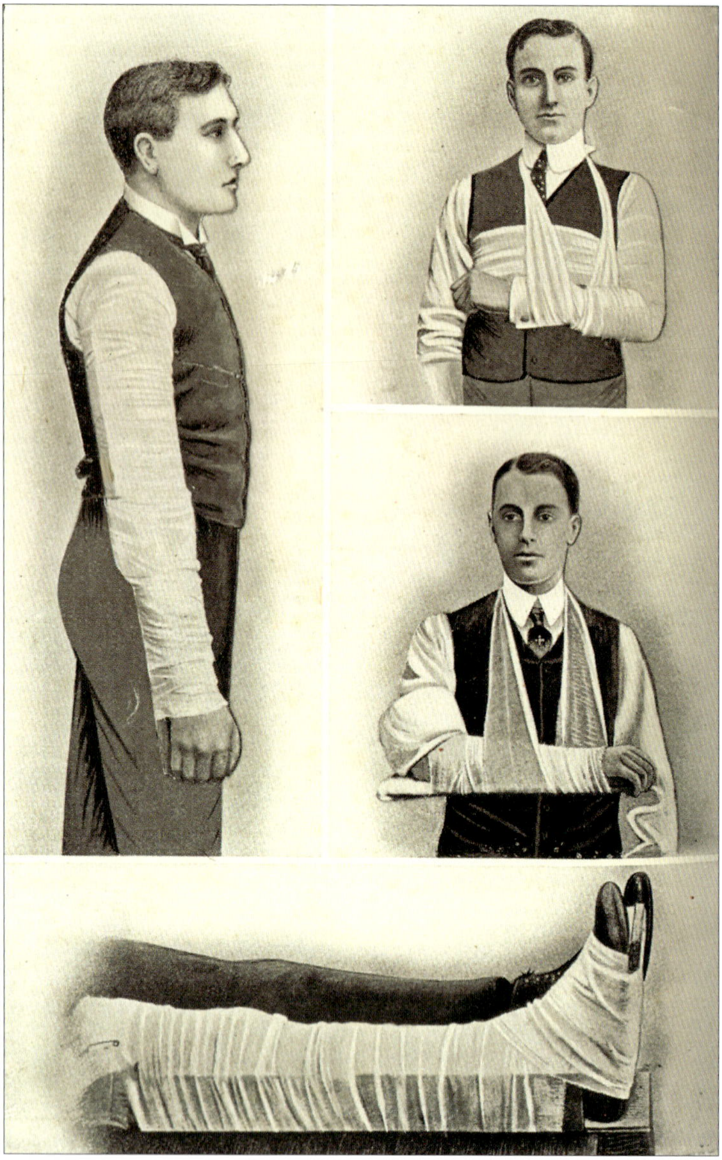

Figure 8
Nursing 3. *Mrs Beeton's Book of Household Management*, London, 1921.

that connects mothers and their infants. There is something about the cultural classification of textiles that is "homely," in the American sense of the word—not beautiful or unsexy—but this anxiety conceals something far more interesting which derives from the European sense of the home as one-half of the antithetical *unheimlich*: the uncanny. It is the uncanny, the troubling anxiety of familiarity and otherness which generates the heightened ambivalence our culture has about cloth and clothes, ranging from the worship of garments as temples of the soul, to contemptuous derision about the "rag trade."[5] That this is as primal as the sexual instincts described by Freud, is evident in the close relationship between the uncanny and the fetish. The need to find the *heimlich* as a form of embodiment and as symbolic representation of the maternal body is as strong as the infantile need for the father's protection, which Freud hypothesized as the strongest need of childhood. The maternal, matrixial, unconscious, emotional, bodily, moving and clinging, precursor of the paternal principle has been described in psychoanalytic terms, more recently.[6] The hand and the eye co-ordinated precede(s) the eye alone, just as the mother and infant fused precede(s) the self as subject. Relation and emotion precede object.

That this primitivism of the unconscious is also to be equated with the style and perspective of the Baroque is another reason why textiles are so interesting, linking the stuff of material culture with the discourses of art history and visual culture. Art historian Wittkower (1958) writes of the conscious aim of the Baroque as being to envelop the spectator in the representational world: "With Caravaggio the great gesture had another distinct meaning; it was a psychological device, not unknown in the history of art, to draw the beholder into the orbit of the picture." The envelopment of Baroque art is a representation of forces felt to be supernatural and divine, and it is only psychoanalysis that has the temerity to suggest that the divine force of God the Father is a matter of a rediscovery, in the supernatural "beyond," of the unspoken corporeal reality of the mundane "before." We can see that the sublime is a before that has been projected into a sense of destiny and destination. Noting, once again, the paradox of indeterminacy and fusion, enfolding or recapitulation of moments along the axis of time, it is clear that there is a parallel here between the recursive inversions of active and passive, subject and object, self and other, proximate and distant, visible and invisible we found in Piero Della Francesca, in tombstone sculpture and in the mundanity of cloth.

The Sublimity of Textiles

Cloth, woven on a loom, incarnates the most troubling of conceptual paradoxes. It is a grid, a matrix of intersecting verticals and horizontals, as systematic as graph paper, and yet it is soft, curved and can drape itself into the three-dimensional fold. Weaving is an activity that is both supernatural/divine and mundane. It transforms the natural materiality of animal, vegetable or mineral into the cultural clothing of humans. It is, in Levi-Strauss' terms, a symbolization of the fact of culture itself. Weaving, like cooking, transforming the "raw" material of nature into the "cooked" language of culture. In weaving, the raw material of animal hair or vegetable fiber is transformed into a medium for human relationship. The loom can be seen as a frame, portal, or aperture which opens through the two-dimensional world of surface into the third dimension of space. The analogy between the frame of the loom and the picture frame of painting is significant here, as the frame is the device which facilitates the change in the spectator's point of view from looking at the world to looking at a surface, for meaning. The fact that painting has settled into a tradition of paint on canvas, stretched over a wooden frame, is also significant. The textile of the canvas is the veil drawn over the real which enables the imaginary of art to take its place, as semiotic, representational world.

That space has always, historically and ontogenetically, tended to be corporeal, an anthropomorphic space, the "second skin" of clothing that literally and metaphorically envelops the body and the self, within the orbit of meaning, the furnishing of religious, ritual or domestic space. The loom, viewed as aperture or portal, allows us to explore the contradictory status of textiles as cultural practice and the trouble that textiles cause for cultural criticism and analysis. Like the culinary arts the textile arts combine the ambivalence that accrues to arts that are too proximate to be accorded the prestigious status of distant "object." This proximity is one of emotional not technical reality, and is a question of the uncanny indeterminacy of activity and passivity, of singular and plural, of verb and noun that troubles the illusory surface of language. It makes a symbolic disorder and tangled web of what Jameson (1972) would call the "prison house of language." The rectangular structure of the loom, supporting a grid or matrix[7] of horizontal and vertical threads, begins as Euclidian order and ends as folds of stuff, reversing the biblical genesis which ordains that chaos shall be made into order. It defies the law of God the Father: is there something demonic about cloth?

The cross as archaic human symbol unites the horizontal axis with the vertical, as two different axes of reality. Intuited as a graphic representation of difference, intersecting lines are among the most primitive of markings. It is the point where the arbitrary characteristic of line is transformed into the determination of an intended, authored mark. It is a meaning. Whereas line may be unintentional, natural, and without meaning, the intersection of lines across an axis denotes intentionality, even negation. X is the signature of the one without writing, X is a crossroads, where Oedipus fulfilled his destiny of parricide and X, as every child knows, "marks the spot" where there is buried treasure. The first significant phoneme in the game of presence and absence, the fort-da game of phonemic opposition, is a play on affirmation and negation. The significance of the cross as a marker of negativity, of deletion is transhistorical. It is found in the iconoclasms that accompany religious wars from antiquity onwards, as well as in the crosses that indicate a wrong answer in school work. To score or scratch is often the method of deleting and crossing out, but the history of iconoclasm is rich with examples (Besancon 2000). The first intentional signifying affirmation is a negation, a saying "no" and this meaning is retained in the significance of intersecting lines. The cross is an intentional point in space. We encounter intersected vertical and horizontals again in the axes of the synchronic and diachronic, sometimes called paradigmatic and syntagmetic axes.[8] These refer to the intuited difference of the reality of space, conceived as vertical, and time, conceived as horizontal. For Kant the facts of space and time are the determining characteristics of reality, whereas for the Levi-Straussian the fact of language, and thus society, is as primal as the reality known to philosophers. Before structuralism, religion represented, in purely visual form such as in the cross or crucifix of Christianity, the riddle of geometry and the inchoate yearning or visceral need for some sense of order and division. The cruciform mark abstracts the combination of an acceptance of the material world of earth and its horizon with the striving of the ascensive world of the sublime. Today, even with the spiraling logic of fractals, the grid represents the pictorial representation of rationality, familiar from the geometries of classical architecture through the modular aesthetic of modernist building and town planning. The lines on which we learn to write are inverted and superimposed into the squares with which we learn to add and subtract. The grid structure of Manhattan's streets and the serried ranks of Roman or Nazi battalions are images of the human impulse to control, order and classify, to tame the wilderness. The right-angle is the foundation of the statistical table and it is the smallest structural and signifying unit of woven fabric. It is the basis of what Pennina Barnett, citing Michel Serres, identifies as "box thought," and yet it is also the smallest unit of the fold of soft logic.

Then the loom makes of this grid a woven fabric, simply by threading a continuous line horizontally across, through, over and under, backwards and forwards, in rhythmic repetition to form the warp and the weft of the cloth. Weaving is a digital process: a thread is either above or below another (Jefferies 2000). Like all signifying systems, weaving transforms the analog into the digital. The analog of continuous thread becomes a textile, and the textile then replicates a mimesis of the analog; it drapes, it clings, it folds, it moves. The action of this simple craft turns the grid into matter, material that has length as well as width. Weaving, that feminine[9] craft, has resolved the human paradox of the incommensurability of two different dimensions of geometry and has transformed the most unthinking of animal activity, repetitive movement, into the most thoughtful of human actions, to cover, conceal, protect, display and shroud, in other words to create a "second skin:" to clothe. Not only has the mundane (in the sense of terrestrial, *mondaine*) technique of weaving solved the problem of the sublime, by means of the intersecting cross that unites contradictory vectors, but it also has transformed the Euclidean grid into the Baroque fold. The humble craft of the weaver has morphed the linear into the three-dimensional. It defies the distinction between pictorial and spatial cultures. Fabric, and its technologies of fabrication, I suggest, present such a challenge to the conceptual economy of post-Enlightenment rationality that it has become what Mary Douglas and Edmund Leach call "anxiogenic." It defies classification and thereby calls into question the validity of the classificatory system itself. It is this ability of textiles to disturb the "correct" ratio of symbolic to semiotic meanings, to confound the laws of proportions that make them such a fertile matter for cultural analysis. I want to explore the ambivalence which characterizes our distinctions between classifications of knowing and making. From classical antiquity onwards the sublime has always been characterized as a movement upwards, *sublimine* means "towards the lintel" in Latin, and the ascensive nature of the feelings that transcend pleasure and containment are described, by philosophers of the sublime as complex admixtures of ecstasy and terror. I suggest that making, with its origins in the body and its movement in work is the basis of the *ec-stasis*, and that this knowledge that derives from making, from working with the body, is a component of the sublimity of textiles.

Adrian Stokes suggests:

Our relationship to all objects seems to me to be describable in terms of two extreme forms, the one a very strong identification with the object, whether introjective or projective, whereby the barrier between self and not-self is undone, the other a commerce with a self-sufficient and independent object at arm's length. At all times except the earliest weeks of life, both of these relationships, in vastly differing amalgams, are in play together as is shown not only by psychoanalysis but by art, since the work of art is par excellence, a self-sufficient object as well as a configuration that we absorb or to which we lend ourselves as manipulators. The first generic difference between styles lies in the varying combinations by which these two extremes are conveyed to us. Here is to be observed the fundamental connection of art with the culture from which it arises, for art helps us both to identify with some aspects of our culture, to incorporate or to reject them, and at the same time to contemplate them as if they were fixed and hardy objects.
(Stokes 1978)

Stokes' fundamentally Kleinian psychoanalysis enables us to differentiate a Baroque perspective of folding and enveloping from a more distanced relation of "commerce" that could, if used defensively as denial of interrelation, be characterized as fetishistic. The fetish is any object, but commonly is a body part or garment, endowed with special magical or sexual significance. It keeps malign forces away and is desirable, or indispensable as a presence, to guarantee safety, invulnerability, omnipotence.

The concept of fetish has an interesting use in traditional art history, used primarily in its anthropological sense to demarcate primitive visual culture of magic, amulets and fetish objects from European civilization. The *Encyclopaedia of World Art* (1950) noted that "Fetish objects may take the form of stones, sticks, skins and the like, with incisions and designs but the typical example is the skin bag containing various elements prepared by the witch doctor." By the twenty-first century the assumed neutrality and superiority of European civilization is overturned and the fetish is discovered as an essential dynamic of art, that bag containing the elements prepared for us by the "non human" we nominate as artists. Whether or not textiles are more or less fetishistic, as art object, than those of painting, sculpture, installation and new media is a question worth exploring. Film, because of its heightened use of the gaze and sight, has been discussed in terms of fetishism for some decades, and allied arts in visual culture have adapted, as far as possible, the concepts derived from film studies. We now use a concept of the fetish developed by psychoanalysts such as Freud, Lacan, Robert Stoller, Phyllis Greenacre, Joyce MacDougall and Janine Chasseguet-Smirgel which describes the fetish as an unconscious psychic object: a symbolic representation of an imaginary organ, the penis, that is perceived to be missing from the mother's body. The fetish is an object that stands for that missing penis; it can be an image, relationship, fantasy, story, *mise-en-scene*, smell or texture, but it is first and foremost a way of knowing or believing, that has the function of eliciting unconscious sexual desire, and without which satisfaction or orgasm is impossible. Located, in metapsychological terms, somewhere between the psychoses and the neuroses, the fetish represents the fantasy of being simultaneously joined with, and separated from, the maternal body. It is a paradoxical and impossible object, an unconscious belief, or fantasy, that the mother is phallic sustains an infantile desire to retain omnipotence through being in contact with, or identified with, that phallic mother. That the fetish may be a body part, or something related to a part of the body is a sign of the perverse subject's desire to maintain an illusion of closeness that, paradoxically, sustains a fantasy of being self-sufficient. Fetishism sustains a distance, created through sight and the gaze, which is actually a denial of loss, separation and difference. As Greenacre (1953) puts it "Fetishism is a picturesque symptom."

As a way of relating this concept specifically to textiles I want to describe an encounter between Peruvian cloth and European culture. The woven textiles were considered to have magical properties, and the European narratives projected onto the Peruvian culture demonstrate the fetishistic technophilia of the European neo-colonialist imagination. It raises the question of which culture is the most primitive?

Some readers, those of us *d'un certain age* perhaps, may remember a cult book *Chariots of the Gods,* written by Erich Von Daniken (1998), a German cultural archaeologist who visited the

Nazca plains of Peru, saw there the mysterious line markings on the plains, and "knew" instantly that these must have been made by spacemen who landed there two thousand years ago. Twenty-five years later, despite the evidence produced by the meticulous work of local anthropologists and archaeologists who have excavated the site, Von Daniken is still convinced that the "geoglyphs" as the vast line markings are called, must have there origins in outer space. The alternative explanation is that they are one component of an important prehistoric culture of woven textiles. The markings, made by removing the dark stones covering pale sand, show up as linear designs depicting shapes: a monkey with a spiral tail, a bird and an insect, strangely stylized forms that are also found in the woven textiles excavated at the site, suggesting a particular significance. Facts available to Von Daniken but rejected by him are that the highly symbolic human significance of the designs is also suggested by the ritual sacrifice of the woven textiles, wrapped and buried in underground tombs. Contemporary Peruvian anthropologists and archaeologists have excavated many of the other artifacts from this site and deduced that the Nazca plains were once the site of a city, built expressly for the housing and training of the "priests" of the religion practiced by the Indians that inhabited this plain. It was a religion in which the weaving and ritual use of woolen textiles played a central and critical part. The civilization had no wheels, hub or spindles but nevertheless wove extraordinary textiles of complex design and enormous scale, some six meters wide and tens of meters long, woven of continuous thread up to twenty-six kilometers long. The colors and patterns used are differentiated according to regions and origin. The role of the textiles had never been suspected before, but the role of the immense and visible geoglyphs had been the subject of decades of speculation by European visitors. Other cultural anthropologists had speculated that the markings might have an astronomical significance, like Stonehenge, used to calibrate the movements of the stars and planets for ritual or agricultural purposes, to try and predict seasons, weather or rainfall perhaps. Van Daniken, who was, like others, struck by the great scale of the markings, argued that as the geoglyphs can only be perceived, as a gestalt, when viewed from high above the land; as if from a "God's eye" view, that this spectator position must have been occupied by a perceiving agency. This led to speculation that the ancient Peruvian Indians might have been hot-air balloonists, like some European aristocratic gentlemen scholars, and then to the hypothesis that cosmonauts from outer space must have made the markings as cosmic runways for their spacecraft. The speculation was, and is, an interesting amalgam of the projection of modern European fantasy onto the surface of a pre-industrial, agricultural, society whose inarticulate poverty is unobserved by Von Daniken, and simply becomes a screen for Von Daniken's neo-colonialist fantasy, a mise-en-scene for an imaginary meeting of technological superiority with primitive humanity. It took decades of careful archaeological excavation, collection and cataloguing in the archives of the regional museum, to find that the solution to the mystery lay not in the heavens but in the mundane: in daily work. The daily work of making thread from llama wool, dyeing and weaving it into ceremonial cloth was the most important ritual of the culture. The significance of the artifacts and representational systems of the religion lay in the significance of the technologies of weaving. The scale of the geoglyphs that had led Von Daniken to think of cosmic solutions was simply arrived at by the same process of scaling up that the weavers used, and still use, to transfer a small design onto a textile woven on a large loom.

The substitution of magnitude for significance is still a very common, and very curious, mistake. It was also connected to the misapprehension that something that resembled land art (such as the Great Western Salt Works or a Christo performance) must be more significant than an ordinary craft technique that was being practiced every day all around the German archaeologist whose gaze was turned to the skies. Preferable to spinning and weaving were ideas of astronauts, spacecraft and beings from outer space. The answer lay in the crafts, or labor, that is considered, today, to be "women's work," low in the imaginary hierarchy of the bodily apparatus that ranks the cerebral and visual knowledge above the hands, muscles and limbs, and that does not notice the meaning of work. As weaving is now considered feminine labor, coterminous with the body it was invisible to the mind of mankind, the answer was sought in the stars.

It has been noted by many, such as structural anthropologist Edmund Leach, that mediating categories are especially prone to be split into idealized and denigrated categories. The concept of masculine cloth is one such mediation of antithetical ideas and is often found in either debased, ridiculed form such as the transvestite queen, or in idealized form of priestly robes and sacred cloth. Freud's idea that weaving is unconsciously associated with the grooming or civilizing of hair and the sexual connotations of hair, or of our bodily animal nature, and as such represents the maternal axis, accounts for the anxiety of castration and the fetishistic defense that permeates the cultural gendering of textiles. The masculine is defined in its capacity to separate from, and take its distance from, the maternal. For the masculine to be brought

Figure 9
Cloaks of many colors throughout the centuries. *I See All, Picture Encyclopaedia* Vol. 2: Arthur Mee, London, 1924.

Figure 10
Ecclesiastical cope—a robe of dignity and authority. *I See All, Picture Encyclopaedia* Vol. 2: Arthur Mee, London, 1924.

into contact with the discarded maternal is for contact to become dangerously close to contagion and pollution. The sublime is brought into contact with the mundane.

The Pedestrian Sublime

Once local anthropologists had challenged Von Daniken's misapprehension over the significance of the scale of the markings, further questions remained. The geoglyphs of the Nazca plains are all made of one single, continuous, unbroken line. Although the sandy soil that comprises the pale lines is too friable to support any vehicle, the lines, unobstructed on open plain, are good footpaths. Peruvian anthropologists suggest that they are likely to have been made as ritual walkways like the labyrinth at Chartres, and mazes are used, as a metaphor for the unknowability of life's "grand plan." The significance of walking as a symbolic act carries a wealth of unconscious meaning. Some of the lines are straight walkways between cities on either side of the Nazca plain.

The unbroken lines which depict the monkey and other figures also caused much speculation until the ritual significance of textiles was understood. The paths were certainly made this way because this was, and still is, the way the textiles were woven, using continuous and unbroken thread spun from llama wool.

The thread of life is a metaphor because we find meaning through the technologies we use. Life's "rich tapestry," Shakespeare's metaphor that time knits up the "ravelled sleeve of care" are among many metaphors in the English language. Mourning is often symbolized by shrouding, veiling and covering with drapery which conceals, and evokes the invisibility of those we love but who we no longer see. Shrouds and cloths of mummification also testify to the intensely symbolic meaning of the drapery of separation and the reparative impulse to clothe and protect, to cover the wound and the social fabric that is rent by death. From the single thread to the interpenetrating lines of warp and weft that constitute woven fabric we see the symbolic representation of the individual and the social fabric. A tear or rent in the social fabric is a tactile metaphor for a collective trauma or destruction. The reparative functions of darning, patching, mending are powerful evocations of a cultural need as much as a functional one; the British post-war "Make do and Mend" campaign was as ideological as the wartime sacrifice of garden railings and pots and pans "for the war effort." Reparation, according to Melanie Klein is the universal human response to knowledge of our capacity for destructiveness, and is the basis of art and culture.

For Klein's student, Wilfred Bion, the line represents thought and has a phallic dimension, as do the lines that make up the signifiers of the graphemes of writing. The Kleinians have also suggested that the phallus has the unconscious meaning of "linking," and this finds conscious expression in the concept of family lineage, and the genealogy of patrilinearity where link is nominated through the father's name. For Bion the circle and the dot have maternal meanings while the line is symbolically evocative of the penis (Bleandonu 1993). The signifier as the material presence of meaning, the emergence of sense from the world of sensation, is the condition for what Julia Kristeva (1987) calls the "father of personal prehistory."

Winnicott suggests that the curtain represents repression, a suggestion that is richly fertile for understanding the function of the curtains in theatre, and their vestigial remains in cinema, as they ritually close and open before the main feature is projected. The significance of the curtains that are the central object of Vincente Minnelli's melodrama *The Cobweb* (MGM, USA 1955) is rendered absolutely transparent when read through Winnicott's interpretation.

The wealth of meanings that are found in the everyday metaphors derived from our physical proximity to fabric indicates the extent to which meaning originates in sensation. Sense was not always antithetical to sensibility and in ontogenetic terms it is through maternal reverie that the matrix of "primary maternal preoccupation" (Winnicott 1987) that sensation and physical experience is transmuted into meaning and from there further transformed into language. What remains astonishing about the Peruvian geoglyphs is that their meaning could only be deciphered by rethinking the idealist fantasy of the symbolic origins of thought. Thought has a fundamentally materialist origin. Not so much in Marx's sense of materialism, nor the strictly semiotic materialism of structural linguistics, nor even the looser, more inclusive cultural materialism of the cultural anthropologists, but more in the sense of material as derived, etymologically, from matter, matrix (womb), mother, the psychoanalytic sense of the material reality of emotional and psychic reality, which understands "matter" in the sense of subjectively experienced emotional valence. Something means because something matters. The importance of recognizing this is part of the psychoanalytic project, as the work of analysis, whether clinical or cultural, always entails meeting the resistance of the ego to acknowledging the unconscious origins of its defenses. This resistance is often manifested in a visceral contempt for, and avoidance of, both "touch" and emotional reality. Meaning of ritual artifacts, and the divinities or fantasies that these artifacts signify, arises through habitual movements of the body, and from the body through neurological pathways to the dynamics of the mind. Dance, like music itself is a resonance of sound vibrations in the body, matter moving against matter. Weaving, whether industrial or studio, is a primally rhythmic and repetitive movement. And the ritual walking of the prehistoric Peruvian pedestrian pilgrims also begins to look like an acknowledgement of the mystery of movement sensed but not seen, that exists in the fiber of being, in what Freud calls sex, in the rhythmic experiences of life starting with the baby in the womb, suspended in the amniotic fluid.

There is, then, in the act of going for a walk, a recapitulation of the evolutionary ascendance from quadrupedal to bipedal gait, with its consequent ascendancy of the sense of sight, the origins of ocular centricity of the West as Barnett notes. Also in the humble act of pedestrianism there is a recapitulation of the ontogenetic miracle of the first steps of the toddler, one of the first existential moments when human motor ability matches human ambition and the subject is, for a fleeting moment, divine in its ascendancy and transcendence of rising up from the ground. The ascensive movement of the spirit in the sublime, and in the many different religions which express it, are also forms of this pride in the upright gait.

The connection between the ascendancy of the bipedal gait and the transcendental power of the gaze has been noted by physical anthropologists. The evolutionary mechanism of sexual selection which was once determined by hormonal action and communicated through gesture, behavior and pheromones had created a primate governed, libidinally speaking, by sensitivity to movement and smell. The displacement of olfactory by visual sensation created the supremacy of the eye and of visible secondary sexual characteristics. We know, from Lacanian psychoanalysis, what this meant for phallocentrism as an organizing principle of signification. We know that the triumph of verticality leaves traces in the ego which are superimposed onto the ego cathexis of eye and the gaze. Stephen Jay Gould (1985) notes that there are historical processes that become recapitulated in individual growth. The fusion, in the Oedipal ego, of the triumph of the upright gait, with the magisterial gaze, as the twin signifieds that are connoted within the meaning of the phallus as executive organ of individual will and agency is surely to be understood as one such recapitulatory trace. The mystery is why humanity should mistake the vestiges of a mammalian past with the hope for a technologically sophisticated future.

What is fascinating about this particular kind of nonsense (although all nonsense is fascinating), is the iconic balance that it displays between the economy of knowledge that characterized this kind of popular thought. Von Daniken's thought is not exemplary of all German anthropology, and is more aligned to the crop circles and lay-lines sort of cults, but it is not dissimilar from the economy of knowledge found in perfectly respectable science at the time. For example, Nancy Tanner, American physical anthropologist, demonstrates how the fixed fantasy of "man the hunter" as a group of male hominids chasing big game with sharpened sticks prevented anthropologists from understanding that the earliest forms of tool making and hence language lay in the mother and infant groups hunting for termites with little twigs sticking in termite hills. The rejection of females sitting around catching termites with little twigs while doing childcare in favor of images of adult males together hunting wild animals with weapons is the alternative through which this same misapprehension is found in physical anthropology. It is through this that we piece together an account of the origins of human language and symbol use. The logic of the supplement proved to be the logic of the master narrative.

This is fetishism, the belief that the reified concept of "man" is at the center of a narrative of evolution to progress. The fetishization of technology, such as alien spacecraft, or of virility such as "man the hunter," enabled anthropologists to perceive their object of investigation as artificially self-sufficient and separate from the social and human structure from which it emerged. Like a penis without a body, or to inverse the Deleuze and Guattari hypothesis "an organ without bodies."

Proximity as Insult

As cloth in clothing is the most tactile of surfaces, always in contact with skin and body it carries the contradictory meanings of being an external surface turned outward towards the gaze of the viewer, while remaining forever proximate. Clothes and textiles worn tight to the body, such as Lycra, are especially susceptible to the contempt that is elicited by the insult of proximity.

The insult is a strange and complex one. An insult is a hurt that derives from being not known (*in-savoir*) and the knowledge that is absent is the knowledge apprehended by the exchange of gazes denoted by the concept of respect (*re-specare*, "to exchange gazes"). The tactile can only yield bodily knowledge, that may even remain oblivious to the gaze, and as such it connotes the appetite for contact that is the repressed unknown of the metaphor which inaugurates the realm of the symbolic. As Lacan puts it, "desire-of-the-mother" is overridden by the "name-of-the father," as the signifier takes its place above the signified in the algorithm of the semiotic. Proximity and the touch become the embodied unconscious which is separated from consciousness by the impermeable barrier of repression and the interstitial boundary of the signifying membrane. Language that nominates replaces the finger that points, that is, the index finger. But the noun that replaces gesture will continue to bear the accusatory separation of subject from object with its implicit defense of projection and projective identification.

The hand and its touch become doubly displaced, by the symbolic and by the eye. These two regimes of representation may often be coterminous as Foucault notes in *The Eye of Power* and as Metz and Mulvey have noted in the narrative structure of classic realist Hollywood cinema. Pennina Barnett explores this in the first issue of this journal. The visual often connotes an iconic dimension that carries the meanings of the proximity of resemblance. This gives visual culture a slightly different system of signification from phonemic or graphic language. Although the organization of sensory systems of perception is something that develops gradually, and is to some extent culturally specific, the differentiation between acoustic, visual, kinetic, olfactory and tactile senses will never be absolute. Deaf people "hear" music and the blind "see" because the difference between the senses is something organized by the ego, not the body alone, and there is a complex system of internal communication and "cross referencing" within the ego. This is further illustrated by the primary pre-differentiation that is experienced in aspects of coenesthesia (where one can see a sound or hear a color, or when the information arriving at the ego cannot be differentiated). To some extent, all signification comprises hybridity, and reading entails making complex interconnections between the word as image, the word as acoustic sound as heard, the word as sound that is made by diaphragm, vocal chords, throat, mouth and lips plus the word as conceptual, semantic experience. These different aspects of a signifying system are only separable in theory.

Textiles continue to bear the connotations of the tactile even when they are not worn or made explicitly for bodily contact. A wall hanging, a tapestry, a ritual artifact for symbolic use or the external surfaces of garments such as uniforms which transform appearance into ritual apparition, nevertheless connote the tactile as an implicit meaning. An interesting case is in the ornamental use of surfaces that repel touch and insist on visual incorporation, such as shiny leather, PVC, metallic surfaces and some immaculate synthetics, and these are examples of the disavowal that is inherent in the defense of fetishism. The injunction to look carries the prohibition on touching, and the prohibition carries an implicit acknowledgement of the primacy of the tactile. Every disavowal, says Freud, is an unconscious avowal.

The impact, on the ego, of bodily awareness of movement, is represented through an imago of vitality, the unconscious component of the idea of life itself Thinking arises through making. Thinking is first, and foremost, a fabrication, and the secondary revision of this first action, which works to efface the traces of the work of this fabrication is analogous to the secondary revision of the dreamwork which makes the manifest content of dreams feel complete, seamless, logical and whole.

One of the most misguided conceptions of epistemology that arose from the anxiety of monotheisms, and their cultures, is the belief that thought emerges from inactivity. This belief in the moral superiority of stasis over movement is worth analyzing as it allows us to further understand the ascendancy of optical logic and its corollary, the idealization of distance and fear of proximity, all three of which have bearing on the cultural meaning of textiles. I shall try, as far as possible, to separate out the elements of these different components of this fusion of meanings. Stasis is a necessary precondition for optical spectatorship, and has been coded as post-Renaissance perspective in painting which requires an optically immobile viewer to make sense of the organization of vertical and horizontal lines in relation to the "vanishing point." Not all religious ceremony depends on silent and immobile introspection, some forms of worship are noisy, ecstatic, or comprise a great deal of ritual movement dialogical call and response. The Peruvian Indians practiced both weaving and ceremonial walking in their system of worship. But the form of meditative introspection that has been absorbed into canonical post-Renaissance art, and into the tradition of university scholarship, is one of silent immobility which is supposed to confer emotional containment onto febrile hyperactivity of the mind and body. This tradition is almost entirely unanalyzed although Paul Gilroy once suggested that "Black" culture moves forward through a musical and rhythmic avant garde; that is, that the energies of music and dance precede the organization of experience into other more traditionally symbolic forms such as writing and history. I shall not explore this in great detail here but simply suggest that the reification of stasis may be based on a fear of the ecstatic.

The imposition of a system of control on the psychodynamic mind or the moving body is tantamount to mistaking the secondary revision of dreamwork for the dream itself. By the time that monotheism becomes a psychic, Oedipal constellation, there ensues a subsequent hierarchy that distinguishes types of thinking characterized by "proximity" from those characterized by "distance." This Judeo-Christian belief that contact is contagion and that distance is the precondition for divinity imbues most modern thought and has played an interesting part in the post-Enlightenment classification of cultural forms into a hierarchy of aesthetic and moral order. The sexual arts being close to the body are base and the visual arts that enshrine the optical distance necessary for visual perception are at the apex. There is also a movement, implied here, from the horizontal to the vertical, a metaphor for the fantasy of ascendancy. Not that all sex is lying down or that all art is seen while standing up, but the implicit movement away from the base, carnal, material to the vertical, conceptual and optical embodies a profoundly infantile reality as the means for calibrating the quality of thought.

We are familiar with this hierarchy, it can be found in the idea that spectating circus, cinema, carnival and church is aesthetically inferior to spectating painting, sculpture, theatre and opera. The former, it suggests, implicate an active spectator thoroughly interpellated into the text by the dialogic form of its mode of address, whereas the latter cannot properly be practiced as contact sports, demand observation of the boundaries of the embodied spectator and the autonomous tectual object. The latter are properly bourgeois and the unspeakability of this class vector becomes defensively enshrined in the fetish of "distance."

What are the unconscious components of the anxiety of touch? How is this connection between the unconscious signified of touch, tactility, texture and materiality linked to the "insult" of craft? Enshrined in the semiotic theory of representation is the mechanism of faith in distance. The Piercean concept of the tripartite "levels" of firstness, secondness and thirdness that describe the iconic, indexical and symbolic forms of signifying, illustrates this. The iconic level with its relation of similarity or resemblance between signifier and signified is supposed to be less unmotivated and arbitrary than the distance between signifier and signified that exists in the relationship of synechdotal displacement that is indexical signification. The third, and most arbitrary level is the symbolic in which the rawness of resemblance is cooked through the cultural mediation of systematic separations and the mechanism of language. Just as our table manners separate us from our anxieties of the animal nature of eating and of appetite in general, so semiotic distance separates us from the anxiety that both vocalization and thought arose from the mammalian appetite for proximity.

Because visual culture bears a different relationship to the symbolic from, say, that of phonemic language, it has a different ratio of unconscious to conscious signification. Images, for example, have a higher proportion of iconic (in Peircean terms) than symbolic signification, and they are thus closer to the unconscious than is syntactic language. The passivity of spectatorship, in which the viewing subject is held "suspended" or entertained by the illusion of the image, and its structure of disavowal or suspension of disbelief, is a partial recapitulation of the primary passivity and receptivity described above. While psychoanalytic theories of spectatorship have laid emphasis on the active gaze derived from unconscious scopophilia, and the narcissistic identification inaugurated by the mirror phase, there is a significant part played by primary receptivity which remains obscure.

The obscurity of the pre-symbolic is complicated and fascinating. With textiles in particular the fact that the tactile sense is to some extent merged with the visual means that the embodied meanings of touch and contact are most present in our experience of textiles. The sense of touch depends on movement for its perception. Touch "disappears" when it is continuous and unchanging, and although the meaning of touch is its ability to connote a profound sense of permanence and stability, this meaning is communicated by an experience of transience and movement. Touch can be a caress, a kiss, a hug, a handshake, a push, a shove, a fight, a slap, a punch and these may be actual physical events or metaphorical events. Touch can mean contagion or contamination in some states of mind, and even the most functional of contacts may be experienced as a seduction or as sexual. The antithesis between touch as meaning love, and its opposite of touch meaning control, grasping or possession is another contradiction that is ubiquitous in the connoted associations of the tactile. Freedom and autonomy begin where touch is transmuted from material and maternal reality into metaphorical and relational reality. The meaning of the corporeality of touch spans from the tenderness implicit in a "mother's touch" to the order implicit in the "long arm of the law." These are all bodies in movement. Even the acts of holding and being held entail variations of pressure and modulations of times. Once out of the amniotic fluid the human skin can only experience touch as an intermittent and therefore digital reality. Touch, too, is a language in which the analog of the skin is transformed into the digital of meaning which connotes the analog of timelessness.

There is also much to be said about the association of tight clothes and loose morals. Although there are specific historical changes in couture and style that transcend mores and codes of sexuality, there is something compelling about contemporary associations, particularly with women's clothes, with tightness expressive of an excess of touch considered tasteless and vulgar. To my mind this is not simply an anxiety about display, as is the "striptease" of various degrees of nakedness shown in fashions, but is an anxiety relating to the transgression of the codes of proximity and distance.[10]

Having explored some of the issues raised by the iconic representation of drapery in Piero Della Francesca's Madonna Del Parto, in the myths surrounding the religious rites of the Nazca plain Peruvian people, funereal icons, I conclude with some notes on the use of string in one of Cornelia Parker's works. In 2003, Parker added one layer of meaning to the Rodin sculpture, The Kiss, which has frequently been displayed in the foyer of Tate Britain. The Rodin, a fine example of European romantic and pre-modernist sculpture has, for millions, become an icon of the meaning of Western art as embodying the idealization of sexuality, beauty and love, and this iconicity is used, by Parker, as the starting point for her site specific installation. Parker placed the Rodin in the hall of Tate and wrapped string around it. The string is ordinary, white, domestic string and it is wrapped loosely around the statue in a continuous encircling, enveloping movement, using lengths of tens of meters, casually knotted together to add a layer of "drapery" that is, simultaneously a layer of meaning. The string adds associations of clothing to the representations of the naked adult couple whose sexual embrace depicts the erotic meaning of touch. Parker thereby conveys the domestic impulse to desexualize by "tidying up" and concealing that is a component of the domestic labor of traditional femininity. However, the looseness of the string generates a meaning that is different from the tight ligatures found in, for example, Meret Oppenheim's Ma Gouvernante (1939) which connotes the sadism of binding, the fasces of fascination and fascism, the use of tightness as a means of control. Parker's string is neither the sensible string of a well-wrapped parcel, nor the erotic torsion of perversion, but the loose reverie of thinking. The looseness of Parker's string is associative of a more pensive form of enveloping that suggests the maternal reverie of the relationship between infant and mother where fusion and separation are in continuous process of merging and emerging.[11] One of the meanings of string is that its use, like that of fabric, lies on the threshold between functional "usefulness" with a simple, uncomplicated meaning and its symbolic eloquence as a material for transforming a line into an element of communication; Winnicott notes, in his analysis of a child, the use of string as:

> *lassoo, whip, crop, yo yo string, string in a knot. String joins just as it also helps in the wrapping up of objects and in the holding of unintegrated material. In this respect string has a symbolic meaning for everyone, an exaggeration in the use of string can often belong to the beginnings of a sense of insecurity, or the idea of a lack of communication. (Winnicott 1960)*

In Parker's installation the exaggerated use of string articulates the contradictory thoughts of a spectator's relationship to the primal scene of a sexual union from which she is excluded, except as observer. The Rodin lovers, carved in stone, are so big, so "wrapped up" in each other that they convey in form, as well as in content, the symbolism of the parental couple from which every infant is excluded. The spectator gazing at the art is a medium through which the "infantile gaze" is activated and is embodied. The protective covering veils in the same way as the drapery in Della Francesca's Madonna Del Parto communicates knowledge of the sight of something unconscious or hidden, in this case sex in the haunting sense of the primal scene, and a more inchoate emotion of being excluded, lost, left out and disconnected from these idealized and enormous parents. As Winnicott noted the mood of anxiety about a loss of connection and a disintegration. The tying and knotting in Parker's use of string evoke the controlling and curious gaze of sadism in scopophilia, that Laura Mulvey has noted in film narrative, and the use of the material of the quotidian and domestic, of the "kitchen drawer" to comment on Rodin's masterpiece of idealized romantic love adds an affectionate and witty comment on the feminine and feminist perspective on the masculine tradition of differentiating the sublime and the mundane.

I suggest that textiles are culturally situated on the threshold between the functional and the symbolic and that as such they offer the cultural analyst a privileged access to means of exploring "such stuff as dreams are made of."

Notes

1. The Tourist Information guide to the Baroque churches of Naples described the architecture of the Church of San Gennaro as one of "exasperated fluvials."
2. Serres' work is described by Barnett (1999) in relation to the *Poetics of Cloth as Episteme*.
3. See Jay (1987) on three perspectival regimes.
4. It is possible that this is compatible with the Deleuzian

baroque, the multiplanar perspective of post-Renaissance logic.
5. There is much to be said about the fetish item of the black leather jacket as exoskeleton and carapacem following from Barthes' analysis of the meaning of a collar worn turned up, signifying vulnerability and "insouciance" simultaneously.
6. The Freudian, patrocentric theory of drives and Oedipal structures was significantly reworked in Britain after the Second World War when analysts such as Melanie Klein and Donald Winnicott explored the significance of children, the infantile and therefore the importance of mothering. Concepts of desire were qualified by those of need.
7. Bruno Bettelheim (1964) cites the etymological origin of matrix in womb. Others have noted the etymological links between matrix, matter, material and mother, and interestingly, mattress.
8. Structuralist linguist Ferdinand de Saussure described language as a play of difference in which units of meaning, such as phonemes or words are selected from a paradigmatic axis of categories and combined along a syntagmatic axis of, say, sentences. These are often represented as vertical and horizontal lines.
9. Is this borne out by anthropological analysis? In many cultures, including that of the Indians of the Nazca Plains discussed below, the weaving was an activity carried court by priests. Men who were trained in weaving as part of their induction into priesthood. However the association of cloth with threshold experiences of corporeal boundaries gives it, in our culture, a maternal meaning, which makes textiles liable to become, defensively, fetishised.
10. Mary Douglas (1996) quotes Norbert Elias *The Civilising Process* who claims that distance is used to express formality and respect. "The smaller the physical distance between persons" bodies, the more the intimacy; this is the low respect end of the continuum."
11. A full elaboration of this may be found in Winnicott (1960).

References

Encyclopaedia of World Art Vol IX. 1964. New York: McGraw Hill; p. 374.

Barnett, P. 1999. "Folds, Fragments and Surfaces." In *Textures of Memory: The Poetics of Cloth*. Nottingham: Angel Row Gallery.

Benthian, C. 2002. *Skin: On the Cultural Border between Self and the World*. New York: Columbia University Press.

Besancon, A. 2000. "The Forbidden Image." In *An Intellectual History of Inconoclasm*, translated by Jane Marie Todd. London: University of Chicago Press.

Bettelheim, B. 1964. *Recollections and Reflections*. London and New York: Thames and Hudson.

Bleandonu, G. 1993. *W.R. Bion: His Life and His Work*. London: Free Association Books.

Chasseguet Smirgel, J. 1989. *Creativity and Perversion*. London: Free Association Books.

Deleuze, G. 2001."The Fold—Leibniz and the Baroque"

Douglas, M. 1996. "The uses of vulgarity; A French reading of Little Red Riding Hood." In *Thought Styles: Critical Essays on Good Taste*. London: Sage; p.3.

Doy, G. 2002. *Drapery: Classicism and Barbarism in Visual Culture*. London and New York: I. B. Taurus.

Freud S. 1911. "The Meaning of Antithetical Meaning of Primal Words." *Standard Edition of the Complete Psychological Works of Sigmund Freud* Volume 11. London: Hogarth Press; p. 1052.

Greenacre, P. 1953. "Certain relationships between fetishism and faulty development of the body image." *The Psycho-Analytic Study of the Child*, 8: 76.

Jameson, F. 1972. *The Prison House of Language*. New York: Princeton University Press.

Jay, M. 1987. "On Scopic Regimes." In C. Jencks (ed.) *Visual Cultures*. London: Routledge.

Jay Gould, S. 1985. *Ontogeny and Phylogeny*. Cambridge University Press.

Jefferies, J. 2000. "What Can She Know?" In C. Pajaczkowska and F. Carson (eds) *Feminist Visual Culture*. Edinburgh: Edinburgh University Press.

Kristeva, J, 1974. *La Revolution du Language Poetique*. Paris: Editions du Seuil.

—— 1980. *Polylogues*. Paris: Editions du Seuil.

—— 1987. *In the Beginning was Love; The Psychoanalysis of Faith*, trans Arthur Goldhammer. New York: Columbia University Press.

Panofsky, E. 1964. *Tombstone Sculpture*. New York: Abrams.

Powell, K. "Unfolding folding." In Giuseppa di Cristina (ed.) *Architecture and Science*. Colchester: Wiley Academy.

Rachman, J. 2001. "Out of the fold." In Giuseppa di Cristina (ed.) *Architecture and Science*. Colchester: Wiley Academy.

Robinson, C. 2001. "The material fold." In Giuseppa di Cristina (ed.) *Architecture and Science*. Colchester: Wiley Academy.

Stokes, A. 1978. "The Luxury and Necessity of Painting." In *The Critical Writings of Adrian Stokes* Vol 3. London: Thames and Hudson; p. 153.

Von Daniken, E. 1998. *Arrival of the Gods: Revealing the Alien Landing Sites of Nazca*. Shaftesbury: Element Books.

Winnicott, D.W. 1957. *Playing and Reality*. Harmondsworth: Penguin.

—— 1960 "String: a technique of communication." In *The Maturational Processes and the Facilitating Environment*. London: The Hogarth Press and the Institute of Psychoanalysis, 1987.

—— 1987. *Home is Where We Start From*. Harmondsworth: Penguin.

Wittkower, R. 1958. *Art and Architecture in Italy 1600–1750*. London: Thames and Hudson.

T-shirts, Testimony and Truth: Memories of Violence made Visible

Abstract

In the township of Crossroads, South Africa, a group of Xhosa women artists have created an extraordinary space of female agency and empowerment. This women's group, called the Philani Printing Project, has formed a place where art and feminist politics intersect with political action. This paper considers a series of five t-shirts that Philani artists created to testify to their individual experiences with violence. Worn in the tradition of the protest t-shirts that were donned by anti-apartheid activists in the 1980s, these shirts bear slogans that call upon other people to join alongside the women and speak out on issues such as gender equity, violence against women, and other forms of women's rights. In presenting these works, this article aims to frame Philani artists as political actors who strive to make visible the conditions of their lives by focusing their artistic efforts on the exploitation and survival of Black South African women despite apartheid policies that discriminated against them, and a current environment which in many ways continues to be hostile towards the emancipation of women.

KIMBERLY MILLER
Kim Miller is Assistant Professor of Art History and Women's Studies at Transylvania University in Lexington, Kentucky where she also directs the Women's Studies Program. In 2006, Miller will join the faculty of Wheaton College (MA), where she will hold a joint appointment in the Art History and Women's Studies Programs, and coordinate Wheaton's new Women's Studies Program. Miller's research and teaching interests include contemporary art from South Africa, women's visual culture in Africa and the African Diaspora, and global feminist issues. She is also interested in the ways in which artists use visual culture for the purposes of promoting social justice and ways in which women use art as a form of activism and empowerment.

T-shirts, Testimony, and Truth: Memories of Violence made Visible

By claiming that she was to "declare the truth to the people," Sojourner Truth saw her intellectual and political task not as one of fitting into existing power relations but as one of confronting injustice ... believing that speaking the truth in a context of domination constituted an act of empowerment. (Hill Collins 1998)

In 1998, South African artist Nontsikelelo (Ntsiki) Stuurman created a moving and powerful memorial to her murdered friend by painting the scene of her tragic death onto the surface of a cotton t-shirt (Figures 1 & 2). In painting this image, Stuurman declares the truth of this event; the artist exposes the interior of her friend's home as an act of domestic violence is in progress. Using the t-shirt as her chosen canvas, Stuurman presents the image as visual expression of trauma and mourning. By wearing the shirt on her own body, Stuurman literally enacts a gendered dimension of public memory, transforming her female body from a likely site of violence to one that openly calls for justice against these very acts. In looking at this t-shirt, we

Figure 1
Nontsikelelo (Ntsiki) Stuurman "Say No To Domestic Abuse." Acrylic paint on cotton, 1998. Private collection. Photograph: Kurt Bonde.

Figure 2
Nontsikelelo (Ntsiki) Stuurman "Say No To Domestic Abuse" (detail). Acrylic paint on cotton, 1998. Private collection. Photograph: Kurt Bonde.

watch this event unfold as the artist herself witnessed the crime. Along with Ntsiki, we too become witnesses to murder.

Ntsiki's friend (whom the artist does not name) was a frequent victim of spousal battery and sexual abuse. The moment that Stuurman depicts is the instant when the husband murdered his wife by beating her on the head with a large rock. We can see the family of three—husband, wife, and child—standing together in what appears to be the kitchen. A long table with dining objects and a plant is visible in the background. Behind the male figure a low purple divider separates the family's sleeping quarters from the main living space. Small colorful flowers and green plants outside show a garden that has been carefully tended. A tall tree, full of lush green leaves frames the right side of the house; it has been strategically placed there in order to draw our eyes inward to the living area. The artist also uses vibrant color to catch our attention: the interior of the home is flooded with bright orange which, juxtaposed against the cool purple background, alerts us to the trauma that unfolds. In a dramatic gesture the man, who is significantly larger and physically more powerful than his wife, sweeps his arm over the head of his child as he strikes his wife's head with a large object. Turning away from her assailant and towards the viewer, the woman raises both arms to her head in an unsuccessful attempt to protect herself from his blow. The child, a young witness to this scene, tugs urgently at her mother's skirt.

Because of the close proximity of homes in Crossroads, the South African township in which this scene takes place, events which happen in the interior of one's home are frequently exposed to neighbors and the surrounding community. Stuurman demonstrates this by focusing her attention on the interior space of the home. In doing so, she also effectively engages several of the important issues that have motivated women's rights activists to break the silence about domestic violence (Stuurman 1999). Because it occurs between intimate partners inside the home, domestic violence is frequently seen as a personal or private, rather than a political and public issue. It has been a primary goal of women's rights advocates around the world to reverse this perception. Presenting the crime in this manner, in literally opening up the home and exposing this event for public view, Stuurman breaks down the public/private divide, insisting that this kind of violence is not a private issue (Stuurman 1999).

Furthermore, in creating this t-shirt, Stuurman makes visible women's traumatic experiences which are typically rendered invisible in her own South African society. For example, Stuurman continues to publicize this event by wearing her t-shirt even in plain view of the perpetrator that this work depicts. In doing so, not only does she testify to the existence and prevalence of domestic violence, she also comments on the failure of the judicial system to prosecute and punish offenders. Reminding abusers that they are subject to the gaze and actions of others, her image serves as a warning to perpetrators of "private" offenses that they may be exposed through the vehicle of visual culture. She also engages her audience through the use of text, which is an essential part of this work. Set in bright yellow boxes against a purple and red background, the words "SAY NO TO DOMESTIC ABUSE" command the viewer to take action, rather than just observe this violent scene. Stuurman has made the text in bold bright colors for this very purpose (Stuurman 1999).

Ntsiki Stuurman is not alone in her efforts to expose injustices against South African women through the vehicle of culture. Stuurman is one of a group of women artists who form the Philani Printing Project, a women's artmaking cooperative located in the South African township of Crossroads. Once a sprawling squatter camp, Crossroads is now a black township located in South Africa's Western Cape, on the edge of Cape Town, a city which is otherwise known for its extraordinary wealth and beauty. The township of Crossroads is a space marked by a deep history of forced labor, displacement, violence, suffering, resistance, survival, and women's activism (see Cole and Miller 2003). The Philani Project is an extraordinary space of female agency and empowerment, where visual culture intersects with political action. Primarily concerned with economic survival and with self-representation, Philani artists use artmaking as a vehicle to address and confront social and gender inequalities. They produce handpainted textiles with powerful visual narratives that call attention to their own personal experiences with varied public and private forms of injustice and violence, as they simultaneously call for these conditions of injustice to change.

In 1998 Stuurman worked alongside four other Philani artists, Ncediswa Mantlana, Lungiswa Pikoko, Neliswa Fanteni, and Nomfundo Dyantyi, to create a series of five t-shirts, each one depicting an experience that its creator personally had with some form of violence. Worn in the tradition of the protest t-shirts that were donned by anti-apartheid activists in the 1980s, these shirts bear slogans that call upon others to take action on the issues they depict. Through the creation of these t-shirts, Philani women give visual form to women's voices regarding the important issue of violence against women, as they simultaneously use the t-shirt as a unique public space to help women to recover from, and survive, the very experiences they depict.

This paper considers the importance of this series as works of visual culture in post-apartheid South Africa by considering the subject matter—violence against women—within the context of South Africa's culture of violence, specifically the ways in which black women's experiences with violence have been neglected, silenced, or erased from South Africa's historical record. I will consider ways in which the artists maintain an important dialogue with South Africa's Truth and Reconciliation Commission (TRC) by inserting their own voices into the TRC narrative, which failed to fully include the voices of South Africa's women. Although many other visual artists have responded to the work of the Truth Commission, the Philani works are unique in that the artists both extend and critique the Truth Commission's work by presenting the artists' own life stories in cloth, in the form of a t-shirt. When worn, these t-shirts mark women's refusal to keep silent on critical issues, and become public expressions of trauma and memory, two of Truth Commission's primary concerns. As the artists fill in the existing gaps in the Truth Commission's narrative, this series of t-shirts establishes a powerful counter-narrative to the overwhelmingly patriarchal and hostile public discourse that currently surrounds violence against women in South Africa.

Critiquing a Culture of Violence: Gender Blindness and the Truth Commission

The open declaration of the hidden transcript in the teeth of power is typically experienced, both by the speaker and by those who share his or her condition, as a moment in which truth is finally spoken in the place of equivocation and lies. (Scott 1992)

By focusing their artistic efforts explicitly on women's experiences with violence, Philani artists directly engage with South Africa's Truth and Reconciliation Commission which was also concerned with the representation of violence and the expression of truth through the vehicle of personal testimony. Constituted to investigate human rights violations committed during apartheid, the Truth Commission formed in an attempt to understand the past, to come to grips with the crimes of the past, and to give individuals a chance to tell their stories. With individual healing and national reconciliation as its ultimate goal, the Commission sought to reveal truth through the recognition and recovery of stories that had been previously silenced or ignored. One of the primary goals of the TRC was to compassionately deal with the survivors of apartheid-era violence and to facilitate healing by providing a safe, supportive, public space for survivors to speak.

The response to the Commission's call for confessions and testimonies was overwhelming: perpetrators, victims, and witnesses of apartheid violence applied to appear before the Commission in unanticipated numbers. Extending its deadline for applications several times over a 2.5-year period, the Commission heard testimonies of 7,000 perpetrators of violence and 21,000 victims. When the Commission's five-volume final report finally went to press in 1998, applications for amnesty were still being considered. Eventually, the Commission turned away hundreds, possibly thousands, of individuals wanting to testify. Since the end of the Truth Commission hearings, its final report has been called the "closest thing South Africa has to an official history of apartheid" (Goldblatt and Meintjes 1998). Sadly, women's stories remain largely absent in this new "official" history.

Despite its successes, and its noble attempts at healing a divided and injured nation, the Commission has been repeatedly criticized for the way in which it dealt with women's testimonies regarding their experiences with violence. Beth Goldblatt and Sheila Meintjes, scholars at the Gender Research Project at the University of Witwatersrand in Johannesburg, are two such critics. Goldblatt and Meintjes insist that although the Truth Commission found that "violence has been *the single most determining factor* in South African political history" (Vol. 1 p. 40, italics mine), the Commission failed South African women because it did not attempt to fully understand or explain the gendered nature of apartheid violence. In addition, the Commission did not take into account other factors which would be specific to women's experiences, such as the shame associated with speaking publicly about sexual violence. The consequences of this failure are profound. Not only did many women activists and survivors of human rights violations stay away from the Commission because they felt that what happened to them was either not serious enough or too embarrassing to speak about, but "the failure to utilize a gendered analytical framework ... has led to a number of weaknesses with the report which has [had] serious implications for the telling of [South Africa"s] history" (Goldblatt and Meintjes 1998: 1). This failure to consider gender as a factor in apartheid's human rights violations means that the seemingly "objective" approach to the recording of South Africa's history has instead resulted in what Goldblatt and Meintjes call "gender blindness:" an exclusion of women's testimonies, experiences, and suffering (Goldblatt and Meintjes 1998: 4). Other citizens and scholars share this concern. As Cheryl McEwan points out, because victims' accounts of events often dictate the way that history is remembered and perceived (McEwan 2003), the absence of women at the Truth Commission will ultimately result in their absence in historical accounts of apartheid. The Commission's gender blindness has proved particularly devastating for women's recovery on an individual level, and has had long-term effects on local and national recognition of gender inequality. For, as Goldblatt and Meintjes explain, many women in post-apartheid South Africa continue to "suffer from apartheid policies despite formal legal changes" (Goldblatt and Meintjes 1998: 4).

For example, while apartheid created a particularly hostile and violent environment for black women, who were the most oppressed sector of the population, they continue to be subject to varied forms of violence despite the fact that the new South Africa appears, on the surface, to be one of the most "gender friendly" places available to women worldwide. South Africa's new democratic constitution is one of the most progressive in the world in terms of gender awareness; it contains an equality clause that explicitly outlaws any kind of discrimination based on gender. The new government also boasts an extraordinarily high number of female leaders, and overall, the growth of gender consciousness in South Africa since apartheid's end has been impressive. Despite this, many conditions for women have worsened; physical violence is one primary example. Rape statistics are particularly distressing: South Africa currently has one of the highest incidences of reported rape in the world, and it is estimated that if current trends continue one in three South African women will be raped in her lifetime (Green 1999: 70). In response to this, in July of 1999 local newspapers dubbed the city of Cape Town, "Rape Town," due to a sudden outburst in brutal, and sometimes fatal, acts of sexual violence against women. Indeed, the Truth Commission's gender blindness holds serious implications for South African women today, a fact that is made painfully clear when viewing the stories displayed on the Philani artists' t-shirts.

I believe that it is useful, if not necessary, to critically consider the production of the Philani t-shirts within this context, where violence against women is not only widespread and increasing, but where the political and social environment continues to be an intimidating one for survivors. Whereas the Truth Commission sought truth and justice through a complicated process of spoken confessions, testimonies, and requests for forgiveness, Philani artists seek representational justice within the domain of visual culture. They attempt extend the work of the TRC and respond to its gender blindness by filling in the narrative gaps that were left open by literally visualizing their own experiences, using textiles to express issues of trauma and memory. Their creative efforts in cloth provide an entirely unique form of testimony—one that is visual and worn on the human body, thus calling attention not only to their own individual stories, but also to the ways in which the South African female body has been a site of violence in the past and continues to be subject to varied forms of violence and oppression despite the end of apartheid.

Stories on Cloth

In her t-shirt entitled "Stop Rape in Schools," artist Lungiswa Pikoko responds to the absence of testimonies about sexual violence at Truth Commission hearings. Most survivors of sexual violence were reluctant to tell their stories to the Truth Commission, either because of the feelings of shame and embarrassment that victims often feel, or due to the social stigmization that survivors often experience. As Goldblatt and Meintjes explain, "public exposure of private violation could undermine the stature of women who come forward, given the already tenuous nature of women's status in society" (Goldblatt and Meintjes 1998: 4). As a result, rather than testify to the crimes committed against them, many rape victims have dealt with their trauma in silence and alone. Pikoko breaks this silence by painting a story about rape onto the surface of a t-shirt.

Pikoko's work, which is based on personal experience, presents the school as a site of danger for many South African females (Figures 3 and 4). The artist explains that violence against girls at school comes from two primary sources, both of which she shows in this image: teachers and other children (Pikoko 1999). Lungiswa recalls one occasion where she was beaten by her teacher until her hands became so swollen that she could no longer move them or write (Pikoko 1999). Because of the teacher's obvious authority over his students, Lungiswa felt unable to report this abuse for fear of further violation. She also tells stories of teachers who regularly took advantage of their authority by asking schoolgirls over to their private homes, or by enticing them to shopping malls, where they would rape them. Speaking in the third person, Pikoko adds, "Sometimes the teacher follows you to his office, and locks the door ... or asks you to come clean his house. And then he rapes you" (Pikoko 1999). Despite the prevalence of this crime, students are not likely to report abuse due to a realistic fear of school (and law enforcement) authorities (see, for example Abarder 1999). Pikoko emphasizes that violence against girls at school is not just limited to those authorities who abuse their power, but is frequently perpetrated by young boys as well.

Despite the silence that surrounds crimes against girls at school, this is not a hidden issue. Non-governmental organizations, universities, academic and activists' journals, and even popular media have recently drawn increased attention to this concern. For example, the South African children's rights group known as RAPCAN (Resources

Figure 3
Lungiswa Pikoko "Stop Rape in Schools." Acrylic paint on cotton, 1998. Private collection. Photograph: Angela Baldridge.

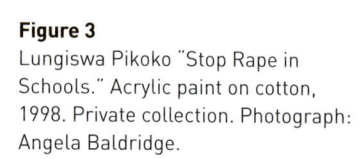

Aimed at the Prevention of Child Abuse and Neglect), has released shocking statistics on the increase of child rape in today's South Africa. Like Pikoko, they identify school as one site where children are most vulnerable to violence. RAPCAN reports that at some schools boys play a popular game called "run, catch, and rape" (Cassiem et al. 1997: 47). Pikoko confirms this: "In schools now boy students grab girls and rape them. School is not a safe place" (Pikoko 1999). In the media, the popular and controversial reality television program Yizo Yizo ("this is it") produced a series in 1999 on problems facing township schools. One of the primary issues addressed was the widespread harassment and intimidation of schoolgirls; the show presented statistics to show that one in three school girls has been sexually assaulted (Garson 1999: 31). In her coverage of the show, Cape Town based Philippa Garson noted, "There's an ongoing daily crisis, pervasive in many of our township schools, which is simply not being tackled with the urgency it deserves. Rape has become a shrug-of-the-shoulders affair" (Ibid.).

In her t-shirt, Pikoko carefully alludes to all of these aspects of school violence. Set against a pink and blue pastel colored background, this image presents an outdoor scene of a township schoolyard. The school building itself occupies the central space in the piece, offset slightly to the upper left-hand corner of the work. Around the school stand several male and female figures, interspersed amid trees of varying sizes. Given the artist's personal experience with this issue, this scene could be a specific schoolhouse known to her local audience. On the other

Figure 4
Lungiswa Pikoko "Stop Rape in Schools" (detail). Acrylic paint on cotton, 1998. Private collection. Photograph: Angela Baldridge.

hand, given the prevalence of this issue in South Africa, it could also represent any township schoolhouse, as no other familiar objects or landmarks are visible in the background to indicate a specific location.

To the right of the work is a young girl. This is her story. Although she is the main subject of the work, Pikoko depicts her as physically marginalized in both position and body size, indicating her emotional state and her lack of physical power. She is afraid and vulnerable. And yet she is not alone: she stands holding onto her mother's hand. As the mother faces and walks towards the schoolhouse, the young girl tries to resist by pulling away; her feet and head both face away from the school, in the opposite direction of her mother's movement. The smallness of her pink dress marks her gender, while emphasizing her tiny body.

Following the mother's lead, the pair enters into dangerous surroundings. The school building itself is presented not as a place where learning is encouraged and where children are safe, but as a site of intimidation, fear, and potential violence. Painted black to signify the girl's apprehension and fear of the place, the building looms in front of the child as a menacing space, casting a far reaching dark shadow on the ground before them (Pikoko 1999). Although Pikoko is not specific about the whereabouts of this particular school, its architectural style indicates that it is likely in one of South Africa's many townships, where buildings are typically constructed by locals utilizing salvaged materials. The wavy line indicating a corrugated iron roof makes this point clear.

Danger also lurks outside the building in the schoolyard; three males of varying age and size surround the school. Two of them stand precariously close to the mother and child, hiding behind a tree while another lurks around the opposite side of the school. All three figures could effectively block the girl's entrance to the school, but she must pass by each of them. Although the figures stand behind trees, or in the shadow of the school, they are also arrogantly in plain view of their victim and her mother; their potential power allows them to show themselves as unafraid to be seen.

It is also important that Pikoko has not given any of these figures facial features, except for eyes, and that she has purposefully distorted their bodies. The male figures in particular are roughly drawn. Certain body parts, like their arms, are enlarged to suggest the potential to assault, while other body parts like heads and torsos are minimized or completely absent. This effectively dehumanizes the figures, suggesting that those who are capable of committing rape, especially against a young girl, are not fully human. The erasure of facial features on the females serves an entirely different purpose. While experiencing rape can also be a dehumanizing experience for the victim, Pikoko purposefully protects the identity of the females in this image by refusing to show facial features, thus maintaining confidentiality and protecting them from the stigmitzation that accompanies rape. In this oppressive image, Pikoko presents this girl as entering a violent environment from which she has no recourse, little safety, and few ways to protect herself.

When I asked Lungiswa Pikoko how she personally dealt with the threat of violence in her life, five other artists responded almost simultaneously, and an energetic and engaged discussion ensued. The artists spoke about the lack of safety in their community, and discussed the actions women can do to try and prevent rape, given the environment in which they live. One artist commented that in Crossroads, it is "not safe to wear short skirts," but then another artist quickly added that "even long skirts don't protect us." Pikoko lamented, "I don't know how to protect myself. Even if you wear long dresses and long tops, if someone wants to rape you they will" (Pikoko 1999). Ntsiki Stuurman angrily said that there is no more respect for women in Crossroads, and that even elder women are regular targets of sexual violence. "I don't feel safe anywhere, anymore" (Stuurman 1999). Several artists connected their fear of rape to the fear of HIV/AIDS, in part because of the social stigma attached to AIDS in many South African communities. "We are afraid of people with AIDS" (Stuurman 1999). All of the women agreed that a belief in God and the act of prayer were two of the only things that women could actively do to help themselves.

This discussion testifies to the pervasiveness and devastating power of what may be called South Africa's "rape culture." A rape culture is one that accepts and perpetuates sexual violence. Pikoko represents the horror of South Africa's rape culture from a schoolgirl's perspective. Although the position of women within a rape culture is often that of victim, there are several important ways for women to resist and respond, ways that are critical for survival. In order to survive within a culture of violence one can do two things: respond and testify. In creating this t-shirt, Lungiswa Pikoko successfully responds to rape and testifies to particular experiences of schoolgirls by calling for an end to rape at schools. She does this not only through the creation of the image, but in the brave way that she combines image and text together in this work. In Pikoko's image, the silence surrounding this issue is most clearly represented by the striking absence of facial features on all of the figures. The most troubling implication of this is that the young victim is unable to call for help, or to talk to others about the experience. It also indicates that both perpetrators and victims are unable to communicate with each other, or with others, except through acts of violence. However, this silence is countered by Pikoko's use of text. Signing her full name alongside the right edge of the design, closest to the body of the young girl, Pikoko suggests that this work is an act of personal testimony. At the bottom of the image she demands, "Down with rape at schools." There is no misunderstanding the content of this work, or the bravery of its author.

Pikoko's personal testimony is as political as it is artistic, especially when considered against the backdrop of the Truth Commission. For not only did female survivors of sexual violence tend to keep silent during Truth Commission hearings, but the Commission's Amnesty Committee did not include crimes of sexual violence in its guidelines for eligibility. Amnesty required that the "act, omission or offense to which the application relates is an act associated with a political objective" (Coleridge 2000: 3), and more often than not rape could not be proven to have been motivated politically. As a result, not one individual amnesty applicant confessed responsibility for crimes of sexual violence. This indicates that in the eyes of the government, these crimes are inconsequential to national reconciliation and healing. Yet knowing that personal testimony is indeed crucial to survival, recovery, and justice, Pikoko's creation not only legitimizes her experience, it also helps to set the record straight in recording the pervasiveness of this crime. The creation of the t-shirt is a powerful strategy to publicize the discussion of sexual violence.

Like Pikoko, artist Neliswa Fanteni locates her scene in a specific space where women are likely to experience violence, and where their vulnerability is increased by their virtual invisibility in the public eye. In her shirt entitled "Farmers must stop the abuse of women" (Figures 5 and 6), Fanteni calls our attention to violence against women in the workplace, with a focused concern on women field laborers at local vineyards surrounding Cape Town and Crossroads. The township of Crossroads is located approximately 20 miles from South Africa's wine country; it is a lush, beautiful, and extremely wealthy area that is frequently visited by tourists from all over the world. Crossroads' close proximity to the wine lands has made it a source of cheap labor, and most wineries employ women from Crossroads and the surrounding areas as field laborers. This thankless work is both physically and psychologically demanding; done under extremely harsh conditions during the hottest months of the summer, women field workers typically work long hours for minimal reward. They are frequently subject to varied forms of abuse. In fact, South Africa's Commission for Gender Equality has recently identified women farm laborers as a particularly marginalized and vulnerable constituency (Gerntholz and Sunde 1999: 34). Liesly Gerntholz and Jackie Sunde describe women farmworkers as a constituency in desperate need of social and legal protection, adding that the current government has displayed an alarming lack of commitment to women's needs in these areas (Ibid.). Indeed, there is little legal or social recourse available for women who find themselves subject to the kind of abuse depicted in Fanteni's design.

Fanteni responds to Sunde and Gerntholz's call by making the experiences of women farmworkers visible. Like the other t-shirt designs, Fanteni's is based on her own personal experiences as a

Figure 5
Neliswa Fanteni "Farmers Must Stop the Abuse of Women." Acrylic paint on cotton, 1998. Private collection. Photograph: Angela Baldridge.

Figure 6
Neliswa Fanteni "Farmers Must Stop the Abuse of Women" (detail). Acrylic paint on cotton, 1998. Private collection. Photograph: Angela Baldridge.

farm laborer (Fanteni 1999). Before she trained as an artist at Philani, Fanteni worked at a vineyard in the nearby town of Stellenbosch. At the time this was her only option for employment. While laboring, Fanteni was frequently subject to the abusive whims of her employer. She vividly describes working long twelve-hour days in the extreme heat, frequently without any water or rest. Because it was a constant struggle to find reliable transportation to and from work, her daily commute both lengthened Fanteni's workday and added a considerable amount of stress to the situation. When she arrived late for work, her employer beat her. When her rate of work slowed down as a result of exhaustion, her employer beat her again (Fanteni 1999). Fanteni recalls feeling terrorized by the constant possibility of physical abuse. At the same time she was reluctant to resist her employer, for she knew that to resist could mean losing her job and thus her only source of income (Fanteni 1999). After finally leaving her vineyard job and finding employment at the Philani Project, Fanteni created this t-shirt as a form of resistance.

This scene is Fanteni's visual interpretation of her own experience working in the Stellenbosch fields. Showing herself as the small female figure in the top center of the work, her size indicates both social status and her physical state as a laborer. As a black female laborer she possessed no worker's rights or union protection; because of this she shows herself exhausted after having worked many hours without rest. Fanteni describes feeling as if her body had shrunk at this moment, due to both fatigue and fear (Fanteni 1999). The source of Fanteni's fear appears to the left, in the looming male figure of her boss. Rising up beside her, his threatening figure cannot be ignored. Standing in a commanding pose, his left arm grasps a long sharp weapon, perhaps a stick or a whip, which he holds out and raises over Fanteni, as if prepared to strike her as she tries to flee. Both figures are shown in profile, a view that allows us to see Fanteni's swelling eye, a traumatic result of the beating. Aside from his size, other factors attest to the power and authority of her boss, such as the pipe that he casually smokes even as he carries out his abusive task. For Fanteni, this indicates that like smoking, the beating is a regular activity that this man engages in without thought, care, or compassion (Fanteni 1999). Fanteni depicts herself and her co-workers as she felt at that very moment: afraid and powerless against the overwhelming figure of her boss. The size of her image reflects this feeling (Fanteni 1999).

Below this pair are several other female figures lined up in a row, working hard picking grapes from scattered vines. Their bodies are depicted as being even smaller than Fanteni's, and their figures nearly disappear into the landscape. Their proportions indicate both the powerlessness and invisibility of these women, and their vulnerability in this particular context. This vulnerability is emphasized by the presence of the powerful boss and the automobile that cruises past them as they work. Drawn to resemble an apartheid Casspir, the truck drives on a road that encircles this scene, suggesting its constant presence as it makes its rounds through the fields and past each working woman. Because it is constantly moving, the truck indicates its regular surveillance of the women, which leads directly to an atmosphere of perpetual intimidation and fear.

Once Neliswa was safely employed at Philani project, she felt compelled to recall and resist this memory by making and wearing this t-shirt (Fanteni 1999). Even though Fanteni shows her boss as an oppressor—his looming figure is clearly one of physical power—her presentation of him is subversive and satirical. She shows him hot with anger and with heat; as he threatens her, his big face swells to the point of distortion. He is literally overheating himself with his rage. In his anger and arrogance, he transforms himself into a monster. She portrays him as lacking human—or rather humane—qualities (Fanteni 1999). When Fanteni tells the story of this work, she laughs at him, ridiculing his arrogance and inhumanity. She also places herself in this work through text, in addition to image, writing her full name alongside the bottom right of the work. Fanteni combines image and text together in her demand: "The farmers must stop abusing the women."

While Stuurman, Pikoko, and Fanteni's stories expose forms of violence that are directed overwhelmingly at women because they are women: domestic violence, rape, and physical harassment in the workplace, two other artists focus on violence that affects all Crossroads residents: issues of housing and commuting. While these forms of violence are not directed solely at women per se, they do affect a greater number of women because of the daily living realities in South African townships, where women are disproportionately victims to violent crimes. In addition, these final two shirts illustrate a gendered phenomenon which occurred at Truth Commission hearings: during their testimonies, men tended to speak about their own experiences with violence while most women talked about violent acts that were committed against others. Women rarely spoke about themselves. These final two shirts address this issue, engaging with the ways in which women internalize violence.

For example, Nomfundo Dyantyi's design addresses the pressing issue of violence within South Africa's taxi industry and the constant effects of this violence on the artist's own life, the lives of her family members, and the entire Crossroads community (Figures 7 and 8). The work engages the complicated politics surrounding minibus taxis. These local taxis, which Nomfundo shows here, have historically been one of the only forms of transportation available for people living in South Africa's townships. During apartheid, the taxi industry provided an important solution to many of the problems faced by the majority of South Africans, especially the lack of quick and affordable transportation to help them travel the long distances from their homes to their places of employment. Taxis offered fast and cheap transportation to township residents on a regular hourly schedule. Because they were locally-run businesses, taxis also supplied a number of unemployed township residents with steady income. This continues to be the case: recent estimates state that the taxi industry now contributes approximately R12 billion (about US$1.3 billion) towards the country's economy each year (Mtshali 1999).

As in other South African township areas, the taxi industry has been of utmost importance to residents of Crossroads. Because of the virtual absence of employment opportunities in the immediate area, many residents are obliged to travel about 15 miles into the city of Cape Town for work and necessary activities such as grocery shopping (although trains are available, many women also avoid using these because the daily violence on them marks them as particularly unsafe for women). Yet because of the escalating violence among competing taxi companies, many people choose to walk this long distance, along the dangerously busy highway, rather than risk a taxi ride. It is not unusual to see women walking the long distance from Cape Town to Crossroads on excruciatingly hot days, burdened with many heavy plastic grocery bags; many women would rather spend an enormous amount of physical energy and nearly a whole day to fetch groceries rather than face the potential violence of riding in a local taxi.

Although taxis have been and still are the most effective means of

Figure 7
Nomfundo Dyantyi "Taxi Violence." Acrylic paint on cotton, 1998. Private collection. Photograph: Angela Baldridge.

Figure 8
Nomfundo Dyantyi "Taxi Violence" (detail). Acrylic paint on cotton, 1998. Private collection. Photograph: Angela Baldridge.

transportation from the township to the city, conflicts have engulfed the industry since its inception, and taxi services have grown increasingly dangerous in recent years. Taxi companies compete with each other for access to routes and the business of commuters, each company seeking market dominance. This competition frequently erupts in the form of violence and bystanders are often killed either near their homes or on the road while taxis are in the process of driving. To complicate the issue even further, because of the lack of police presence and safety in township areas, taxi companies are often called upon by local communities to do vigilante work (Dyantyi 1999). This violence affects a large number of people: Thokozani Mtshali, a journalist for the *Mail and Guardian*, reports that 12 million regular commuters are caught up in the daily fight for dominance among taxi organizations (Mtshali 1999).[1]

As a regular commuter and a witness to outbreaks of violence between competing taxi companies, Nomfundo Dyantyi speaks out against this form of violence in her work. She presents a scene from a specific event where gunfire erupted in Crossroads between warring companies in June, 1997. In the background Dyantyi shows four taxis parked in a row alongside the busy highway that borders Crossroads. The two additional taxis pictured have pulled out of the line and onto exit ramps to be closer to the living areas of their commuters. Each taxi represents a separate company. The one taxi in the foreground is the subject of the work; it has parked closer to Crossroads' residential area and therefore many Crossroads residents, pictured standing in a group nearby the taxi, have chosen to solicit this particular taxi company rather than walk the additional distance to the taxis that wait in line.

The resulting chain of events illustrate Dyantyi's narrative. Two angry drivers from the back row of taxis have approached the lone vehicle in an ambush. They are both armed with guns. One man is shown standing in the middle of the road, shooting a stream of bullets directly into a window of the taxi, while another man is off to the right standing over the body of his victim. Although the fallen man, who was dressed for work in his button down shirt and tie, lies in a pool of blood, the killer continues to aim his weapon at the dead body and bullets can be seen flying from the barrel of the gun. A small child watches this scene. Between the two assailants a crowd of men and women dressed in work clothes attempt to flee the gunfire, as an individual on the far left gestures wildly for them to run in his direction. Most of the commuters escape the hail of bullets but clearly not everyone in this image was so lucky; several individuals were caught in the crossfire and two people were killed. As one of the group of commuters, Nomfundo inserts herself into this scene, bravely presenting herself as an eye-witness to this carnage. Her first name, written directly below the murder scene in the lower right corner of the work, identifies her as artist, witness, and activist; there is no mistaking who she is.

Although Nomfundo freely admits that she is afraid of the taxi violence, she reacts to and overcomes this fear in part by creating this t-shirt and talking about how taxi violence affects her personally. She describes hearing gunfire between warring taxi companies from her home on a regular basis, and reports the grief her friends endured when they heard secondhand that their children had been killed. When questioned, Nomfundo readily recalls other incidents in which she has personally witnessed murders similar to the one in this scene. Yet Nomfundo's anger is more powerful than her fear. Enraged that this crime went unpunished, and tired of living in fear of the potential violence that she faces as a commuter, Nomfundo speaks out about this form of violence by making this t-shirt (Dyantyi 1999).

Along with the other shirts, this image aims to prompt political change by directly confronting the perpetrators of this crime. Seeking to expose the identity of the murderers and wanting to tell others about their acts, Nomfundo printed extra versions of this shirt and subsequently distributed them to taxi commuters, and eventually to the drivers themselves. In an extraordinary act of bravery, Nomfundo actually wears this t-shirt as she commutes, visually confronting the perpetrators of the crime which she depicts. Her Xhosa command is boldly printed along the top and bottom of the work: *Xholoxholo Maziphele* ("stop violence"), and is accompanied by the large yellow dove, as a visual call for peace (Dyantyi 2001).

In this final t-shirt, artist Ncediswa Mantlana depicts the township violence that has recently erupted in the streets of Crossroads over the issue of housing (Mantlana 1999; Figures 9 and 10). In addition to illustrating living conditions in Crossroads, Mantlana portrays the physical violence that occurs as a result of local controversies surrounding the new houses which were built in Crossroads by South Africa's democratic government. Tens of thousands of small, box-like corrugated iron and wooden shacks crowd together here on a narrow stretch of barren land. Government sponsored homes, also small but made from the more durable materials of brick and concrete, are visible in this landscape, appearing in increasing numbers as democratic rule has become a reality in South Africa. The presence of these homes is both welcome and problematic, for although the homes help fulfill a desperate need for permanent, stable shelter, they simultaneously maintain apartheid segregation by transforming a post-apartheid

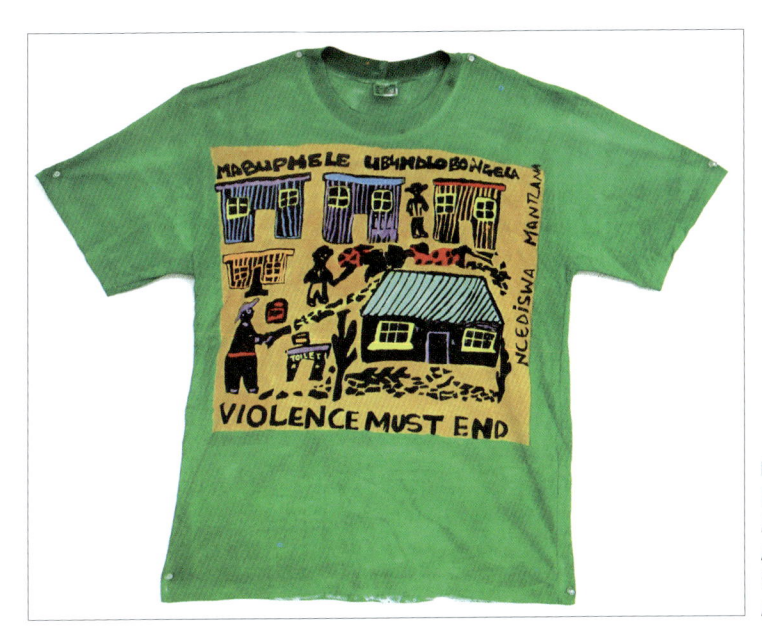

Figure 9
Ncediswa Mantlana *Xholoxholo Maziphete* "Stop Violence." Acrylic paint on cotton, 1998. Private collection. Photograph: Angela Baldridge.

Figure 10
Ncediswa Mantlana *Xholoxholo Maziphete* "Stop Violence" (detail). Acrylic paint on cotton, 1998. Private collection. Photograph: Angela Baldridge.

Crossroads into a permanent black settlement. Mantlana visualizes the contrast between the old and new homes, emphasizing differences in material and color, as well as calling attention to the similarities in size and location: a row of typical informal homes in the background, marked by the box-like structure and flat roof, is juxtaposed against the new, slightly larger, and more permanent government homes in the foreground. These new homes are desperately needed by the majority of Crossroads' residents, for the older, informal shelters are small, and are composed primarily of discarded and easily perishable materials such as corrugated iron and timber. Insecure in both construction and security, the informal homes often lack doors or entire walls, offering limited privacy and making safety a constant concern.

When the ANC came to power in 1994, they recognized this concern. The new government initiated an ambitious housing program in an attempt to provide more permanent shelter and better living spaces for people in communities such as Crossroads. Although many people have argued that access to housing is one of the most successful programs undertaken by the new government—between 1994 and 1999, 959,000 families had been served with housing subsidies and over 680,000 houses had been built—hundreds of thousands families still wait to be served. In addition, there is widespread and justifiable dissatisfaction with the homes that have been built. A staff reporter for *The Mail and Guardian* reports,

> *One criticism of the government's mass housing project is that it has failed to [fundamentally] transform the urban landscape, in that most of the houses have sprung up inside existing townships...*

apartheid planning [continues to] live on into the next millennium in much of South Africa.

Indeed, residents of Crossroads and similar spaces have good reason to be suspect of government promises of "upgrading."

This general dissatisfaction with new housing extends to Crossroads where many residents complain that the houses are too small and that the changes are not significant enough to make a meaningful difference in the lives of most residents. Mantlana emphasizes this in her juxtaposition of the two rows of homes: she illustrates that the new permanent housing does not differ greatly from the informal housing of apartheid years. Although Mantlana shows the government built home is constructed with more permanent materials and is thus a steadier shelter, it is only a slightly larger space, and is insufficient to accommodate the size of most local families. Mantlana has also placed an outdoor toilet stall in front of the new house as a sign of continued inadequate sanitation. Even though this toilet offers residents closer proximity to facilities, this solution is not sufficiently sanitary or private. Echoing the sentiments of many of her neighbors, Mantlana insists, "the government's big house is too small" (Mantlana 1999).

In the tragic event depicted here, the combination of dissatisfaction and the overwhelmingly desperate need for stable shelter have led to violence. Offended by the location and construction of these homes, residents of Crossroads who were selected to move into the new homes relayed their dissatisfaction by staging a boycott. They refused to move as a means of protest, and instead remained in their own "informal" houses, leaving the new homes vacant. Rather than responding to the residents' dissatisfaction, the government offered the new homes to families who were next on the waiting list. When the new families decided to accept the government's offer, and move into the homes, the tragic result was the violent scene pictured here. Standing between a row of three old homes and one new government home, four Crossroads residents fight over this issue. The large man in the foreground, who is one of the boycotters, tries to prevent his neighbors from moving into the brick home by blocking the front entrance and pointing a loaded gun at his neighbors. As he pulls the trigger, a stream of bullets shoots through the houses towards the figures. Blood has already been shed for this cause, as a fallen man can be seen on the ground between the houses, lying in a pool of blood.

This work is grounded in historically specific experiences of housing and violence in Crossroads. Although the perpetrators and victims of violence shown in this particular image are all male, Mantlana considers this kind of violence particularly injurious for Crossroads women (Mantlana 1999). As a long time resident of Crossroads, Mantlana has long struggled for access to space, shelter, and safety; she is acutely aware of how these issues have hit women particularly hard. Mantlana talks openly about how, under the previous government, it was often dangerous for a woman to leave her home. She readily recalls the terror of literally dashing between her home and the local convenience shop, holding on to her children as she ran. As a 35-year old woman, Mantlana lived through the worst years of apartheid violence in Crossroads, and she mourns the fact that despite the end of apartheid, violence continues to erupt in her neighborhood over issues of adequate space and housing (Mantlana 1999).

T-Shirts, Testimony and Truth

To pull on a t-shirt can be an act of courage. (Williamson 1989)

Artists at the Philani Project publicly mark themselves as survivors of and witnesses to violence by creating and wearing these t-shirts. In addition, they continue the unfinished work of the Truth Commission, citing specific events, naming perpetrators and memorializing victims. When viewing their work one cannot help but experience the artists' deep commitment to centering women's stories through public testimony. This form of truth-telling places Philani artists within a long established tradition of black women who have sought personal empowerment and public justice through the act of testimony. As Patricia Hill Collins, who has written extensively about the historical importance of black women's testimonials, says: "a Black women's testimonial tradition [is] long central to naming and proclaiming the truth ... testifying for or publicly speaking the truth, often about the unspeakable, not only recaptures human dignity but also constitutes a profound act of resistance" (Collins 1998: 237–8). In speaking publicly about violence against women, in refusing to be silenced, and in overcoming their own existing fear of violence, Philani artists enact and continue this tradition.

For example, the act of testifying involves insisting that one's private acts be taken seriously as public concerns, for public awareness is crucial in the search for justice. Collins elaborates on this:

> [W]ithin a narrow use of the testimonial, individuals testify within a community of believers such that each testimonial spurs others on to greater faith. However, a broader use of the testimonial involves testifying the truth to cynics and nonbelievers. Within a more generalized testimonial tradition, breaking silence, speaking out, and talking back in academic settings constitute public testimonials. Moreover, linking this tradition to a search for justice politicizes it. (Collins 1998: 238)

In addition to politicizing an issue, public testimony may also facilitate individual healing:

> naming oneself and defining ideas that count as truth are empowering acts. For those damaged by years of silencing, [testifying] speaks to the significance of self definition in healing from oppression... Although important, private naming is not enough—truth must be publicly proclaimed. (Collins 1999: 208)

Through visual testimony the artists discussed here insist that the issues that affect black women be recognized as an integral part of South Africa's democratic transition.

This testimony is also deeply personal, not only because the artists themselves are survivors of violence, but because they use a unique space—a t-shirt worn on the body—as their chosen site. Philani artists seek justice and confront historical silences not just through acts of creation and representation, but in wearing these stories *on their bodies*. As art historian Nicholas Mirzoeff reminds us, the female body is also an important and potentially powerful site of representation: "The body is involved in struggles that are political but are also inescapably issues of representation" (Mirzoeff 1995: 7). In this particular context, the act of wearing the t-shirt on the body also recalls the thoughts of Mirzoeff, who, elaborating on Foucault's discussions on the relationship of the body to larger systems of power, reminds us that "the body was and is a key site of ... resistance [that is] provoked by any exercise of power" (Mirzoeff 1995: 11). Mirzoeff's words are meaningful here, suggesting the sense of empowerment that may result from what may otherwise appear to be insignificant acts. In wearing visual representations of experiences with violence, experiences that they have themselves survived, not only do the artists signal their own empowerment, but each time the shirt is worn it serves as a reminder to all who see it. In wearing their t-shirts, each woman claims power and ownership over her own body in a very visible and very public way, signaling her refusal to live life as a victim.

Philani artists also engage with another important tradition of visual resistance that is historically specific to South Africa: the use of the t-shirt as a form of public testimony and political protest. In creating and wearing these shirts, the Philani artists place themselves within the continuum of South African artists and activists who have bravely worn the t-shirt as a cultural tool to resist oppression and demand social justice. Widely recognized for its ability to quickly and effectively transmit political messages, and to speak to a variety of peoples across a multi-lingual South Africa, t-shirts were frequently used as a cultural tool in the struggle against apartheid. Because they carried and expressed a variety of political messages, t-shirts helped inculcate certain visual slogans, or recognized the policies of martyred political leaders who perished in the struggle for freedom (Williamson 1989: 93). Anti-apartheid activist Don Pinnock has noted the unique political power of t-shirts as a form of popular visual communication, particularly in township areas:

As the news frame of the guild media moved further and further away from township reality, people there [in townships] continued to watch TV, listen to the radio and read commercial newspapers. But increasingly the information which informed their choices and action came from elsewhere: from the popular circuits of communication and from understandings drawn from events around them which together added up to a fundamental social transformation at the level of popular consciousness.
(Pinnock 1989: 23)

Under apartheid rule, the power of t-shirts to quickly and effectively communicate political messages among activists was especially important during increased censorship of the media and the growing government control over literally all forms of public information and communication. The subversive power embedded in this form of visual resistance was not lost on the apartheid state, whose response to the political wearing of t-shirts was to censor them. First banned under the auspices of the so-called Public Safety Act of 1953, political t-shirts were ultimately prohibited by the government under the second state of emergency, which enforced much stricter definitions of what constituted a "subversive statement." Artist Gavin Younge recalls that "Protests as ephemeral as those emblazoned on T-shirts have been considered subversive and have been banned" (Younge 1988: 14). Likewise, artist/activist Sue Williamson, who was once arrested for creating and wearing a women's rights t-shirt (Williamson 1999) recalls, "the humble t-shirt has become a potent way of making a personal political statement" (Williamson 1989: 93). A body wearing such a shirt was a vulnerable body, and a likely target for government violence.

When Sue Williamson said "To pull on a t-shirt can be an act of courage" (Williamson 1989: 93) she was speaking of the activists of the 1980s, who fought for racial justice against an oppressive government. But Williamson could very well have been describing the actions of Philani artists, for like those artists and activists who came before them, Philani artists engage in political action in order to resist oppression in wearing their testimony on their bodies. In this sense they continue the tradition of using the power of visual culture of everyday life to fight a political struggle, although they fight not against an oppressive state, but rather against an entire culture of violence where women are the most frequent victims. As James Scott has said, "The open declaration of the hidden transcript in the teeth of power is typically experienced, both by the speaker and by those who share his or her condition, as a moment in which truth is finally spoken in the place of equivocation and lies" (Scott 1992: xiii). Scott's words are useful here, for as these t-shirts show, for South African women the teeth of power can be located in the government, on the streets, at work, at school, and in the home. The teeth of power are at once national and local, and in expected and unexpected places, including the Truth Commission. In pulling these t-shirts onto their bodies, Philani artists let the world know that Crossroads women want and are willing to struggle for freedom from violence.

Other expressions of protest and pain

A critical analysis of Philani work reveals the artists as political actors who carry forth a global black feminist activist tradition as they strive to make visible the conditions of their lives by focusing their artistic efforts specifically on the exploitation and survival of black South African women despite apartheid policies that discriminated against them, and a current environment which in many ways continues to be hostile towards the emancipation of women.

Note

1. The current government has recognized that taxi violence is a severe problem. Their response has been to try to transform the taxi industry by restructuring it, setting up a national taxi task team to investigate the causes and ways of ending the conflicts within the industry. The government currently offers subsidies to "ensure economic growth and self sustainment of the taxi industry" in efforts to control the violence (Mtshali 1999).

References

Abarder, Gasant. 1999. "Police abandon raped teens." *Cape Times*. February 15

Cole, Josette. 1987. *Crossroads: The Politics of Reform and Repression 1976–1986*. Johannesburg: Ravan Press.

Coleridge, L. 2000. "The amnesty process of the Truth and Reconciliation Commission (TRC) with specific reference to female amnesty applicants." *South African Journal of Psychology* 30: 56–59.

Dyantyi, Nomfundo. 1998. Personal interview, Crossroads, South Africa: December.

———. 1999. Personal interview, Crossroads, South Africa: February.

———. 2001. Personal interview, Crossroads, South Africa: June.

Fanteni, Neliswa. 1998. Personal interview, Crossroads, South Africa: December.

———. 1999. Personal interview, Crossroads, South Africa: February.

———. 2001. Personal interview, Crossroads, South Africa: June.

Garson, Philippa. 1999. "Truth hurts, but it helps." *Mail and Guardian*. 5 February: 31.

Gerntholz, Liesly and Jackie Sunde. 1999. "'Die man is die dak, die vrou is die vloer'—Lobbying for women farmworkers rights." *Agenda* 42: 33–38.

Goldblatt, Beth and Sheila Meintjes. 1998. "Dealing with the Aftermath—Sexual Violence and the Truth and Reconciliation Commission." *Agenda* 36: 7–17.

———. 1998. "A gender persepctive on violence during the struggle against apartheid." In Elirea Bornman, Rene van Eeden and Marie Wentzel (eds). *Violence in South Africa: A Variety of*

Persepectives. Pretoria: Human Sciences Research Council.

——. 1999. "Women: one chapter in the history of South Africa? A critique of the Truth and Reconciliation Commission Report," draft paper presented on 13 June at the CSVR/History Workshop Conference, "The TRC: Commissioning the Past," University of Witwatersrand.

Green, December. 1999. *Gender Violence in Africa: African Women's Responses*. New York: St. Martin's Press.

Hengehold, Laura. 2000. "Remapping the event: institutional discourses and the trauma of rape." *Signs* 26: 189–214.

Hill Collins, Patricia. 1998. *Fighting Words: Black Women and the Search for Justice*. Minneapolis: University of Minnesota Press.

Mantlana, Ncediswa. 1999. Personal interview, Crossroads, South Africa: February.

——. 1998. Personal interview, Crossroads, South Africa: December.

——. 1999. Ncediswa. Personal interview, Crossroads, South Africa: February.

——. 2001. Ncediswa. Personal interview, Crossroads, South Africa: June.

McEwan, Cheryl. 2003. "Building a postcolonial archive? Gender, collective memory and citizenship in post-apartheid South Africa." *Journal of Southern African Studies* 29.3: 739–57.

Meintjes, Sheila, 2001. "War and post-war shifts in gender relations." In Meintjes, Sheila, Anu Pillay, and Meredeth Turshen (eds). *The Aftermath: Women in Post-Conflict Transformation*. New York: Zed Books, pp. 63–76.

——, Anu Pillay and Meredeth Turshen. 2001. "There is no aftermath for women." Meintjes, Sheila, Anu Pillay and Meredeth Turshen (eds). *The Aftermath: Women in Post-Conflict Transformation*. New York: Zed Books, pp. 3–18.

Miller, Kim. 2003."The Philani Printing Project: Women's Art and Activism in Crossroads, South Africa." PHD dissertation, University of Wisconsin-Madison.

——. 2001a. "Truth and the illusion of truth: contemporary South African artists speak." College Art Association, Annual Conference. Chicago, IL, February.

——. 2001b. "Women's art and activism in Crossroads, South Africa: memories of violence made visible." Arts Council for the African Studies Association, Triennial Conference. St. Thomas, USVI, April.

——. 2002. "Art and the Struggle Against Child Poverty in Crossroads, South Africa." College Art Association Annual Conference, Philadelphia, PA, February.

Mirzoeff, Nicholas. 1995. *Bodyscape: Art, Modernity and the Ideal Figure*. New York: Routledge.

Mtshali, Thokozani. 1999. "Taxi factions move closer together". *Mail and Guardian (Cape Town)* 30 April.

Pikoko, Lungiswa. 1998. Personal interview, Crossroads, South Africa: December.

——. 1999. Personal interview, Crossroads, South Africa: February.

——. 2001. Personal interview, Crossroads, South Africa: June.

Pillay, Anu. 2001. "Violence against women in the aftermath." In Meintjes, Sheila, Anu Pillay, and Meredeth Turshen (eds). *The Aftermath: Women in Post-Conflict Transformation*. New York: Zed Books.

Pinnock, Don. 1989. "Culture as communication: the rise of the left-wing press in South Africa," *Race and Class*, 31, (2): 17–35.

Scott, James. 1992. *Domination and the Arts of Resistance: Hidden Transcripts*. New Haven: Yale University Press.

Stuurman, Nontsikelelo (Ntsiki). 1998. Personal interview, Crossroads, South Africa: December.

——. Nontsikelelo (Ntsiki). 1999. Personal interview, Crossroads, South Africa: February.

——. Nontsikelelo (Ntsiki). 2001. Personal interview, Crossroads, South Africa: June.

Truth and Reconciliation Commission of South Africa Report. Vols. 1, 2, 3, 4, 5. Cape Town: CTP Book Printers Ltd., 1998.

Williamson, Sue. 1989. *Resistance Art in South Africa*. New York: St. Martin's Press.

——. 1998. Personal interview, Cape Town, South Africa: October.

——. 1999. Personal interview, Cape Town, South Africa: February.

Younge, Gavin. 1988. *Art of the South African Townships*. London: Thames and Hudson.

Inside out, Outside in: Unfolding a Territory of Process, Material and Meaning

Abstract

The intention behind the following interview was to examine the thought processes embodied by an artwork and the modes by which these might be transmitted to and received by the viewer. Williams often focuses on materiality and the abstract social and/or historical significance. His work considers the associative qualities that textiles prompt in these terms for both maker and audience. The interview was the result of an exchange of emails between Sally O'Reilly and Gerard Williams during spring 2005. It was conducted during the production of a touring commission, Interior Worlds, for *arttextiles* 3, and the initiation of a piece in a medieval tower in rural Lincolnshire for Beacon, and so set out to address relevant issues of context and site-specificity.

GERARD WILLIAMS

Gerard Williams' artworks and associated research over the last twenty years have often engaged with textiles. Most of his recent projects have been place- and/or time-sensitive and have been produced both for and in relation to contemporary art contexts. Since emerging in the 1980s through solo shows at influential contemporary art galleries such as Interim Art and Anthony d'Offay in London, Williams went on to exhibit internationally and to develop a less commercial and more research-based practice which has produced a great variety of outcomes. He was awarded a Henry Moore Institute Research Fellowship in 1998 to examine the use of textiles in twentieth-century sculpture. Gerard Williams is currently leader of the MA Textiles program at Goldsmiths College, London.

SALLY O'REILLY

Sally O'Reilly is a writer and critic. Her practice explores issues that encircle and run through contemporary art, including literary tropes, event theory and the overlap with science. O'Reilly contributes regularly to many art magazines, such as *Art Monthly* and *Frieze*, writes catalogue essays for international galleries and teaches contemporary art practice and theory in universities around the UK.

Inside out, Outside in: Unfolding a Territory of Process, Material and Meaning

Sally O'Reilly: Your work starts very much with the world as it already exists—for example you often react to the demographic of a place or use a shape taken from a very particular situation. Is this a skeptical position, or, if not, how do you stay within the bounds of constructive criticism?

Gerard Williams: You're suggesting that skepticism is used to facilitate constructive criticism? I guess there is an inherently skeptical element to my stance, yes. There's maybe a more precise word, phrase or way of expressing it. The approach is to a large extent about finding a way to question accepted views or perceptions, setting up a relatively simple means by way of which it becomes easy to see, or interpret, the familiar from a different perspective. One that hopefully reveals as much about our preconceived ideas as it does about the starting point for the work.

SO'R: So, rather than skepticism, it is more like the paradox of pessimism: the pessimist, by expecting the worst, sets himself up for some nice surprises, so that it is actually an optimistic position? There is also something about the nature of gallery display that can often transform the interiority of skepticism into finger wagging. You describe your work as interpreting the familiar from a different perspective and questioning preconceived ideas, yet you manage to avoid it being didactic. How do you manage that? How do you pitch the "voice" of the artwork?

GW: I like the paradox of pessimism idea. I don't want to come over as a finger-wagger though. Avoiding didacticism? Hmm. Most presentations of facts or figures or "truth" seem to be formulated for consumption by filtering the source material (for example, statistics through the conventions of some kind of accepted methodology into an established mode of representation (for example, producing anything between a graph and a television documentary). I sometimes make work that is derived from factual information, processing and filtering it as a statistician might, but through an unconventional route using unusual means, devising a route that wouldn't ordinarily be utilized or invented in relation to the kind of information involved.

The outcome (three-dimensional stuff) is correspondingly peculiar, though hopefully logical, perfectly readable and true to the nature of the material represented. This approach aims to get the viewer to consider the source material from a different perspective, as well as to think about the conventions associated with the representation of information. Hopefully, the work then circumnavigates what might be ordinary channels of approach to the subject, avoiding the problem of producing didactic results. I hope there is a space for the viewer to inhabit between the source material and the physical outcome. That space is theirs and somehow should open up the piece on a personal level. Perhaps the viewer is thrown upon their own resources, to an extent, because the use of stats in relation to the outcome as unusual. But now I feel that I've perhaps avoided the element of subjective choice implied by your words "pitch the voice of the artwork".

SO'R: Maybe it is useful to think of your work in terms of a knowing naivety, if that isn't too much of a tautology. When I say that you start with the world as it exists, it's more a case of starting with statistics that reflect an interpretation of the world or, as you say, conventions of some kind of accepted methodology. For example, in your piece *International Trade Fair* (Figure 1), made for the 2004 Frieze Art Fair, you used statistics on per capita GDP, sourced from the CIA website, as a way of building a picture of the countries represented by galleries present at the art fair. As I recall, you used printed fabric flags over which you stitched bar chart-like strips to incorporate the statistics into the graphic scheme of the flag. This is an ambivalent gesture that is both naïve and knowing, critical and helpful. Critical in pointing out the obvious skew of something like the art fair and helpful in prodding us to think that this is a questionable situation, to say the least. What I mean by "pitch of voice" is this ambivalence, which avoids tipping into tub-thumping.

GW: Tub-thumping is not what I'm at! The pitch is definitely ambivalent, as you describe. I guess that it's a particular voice that is made possible by the position of the artwork. People expect to have to adjust their tuning, to observe, think or stand aside momentarily from their habitual ways or society's methods of regarding

Figure 1
International Trade Fair 2004.
Dimensions: flags 10 × 15 cm; installation dimensions variable. *International Trade Fair* was made for the Parker's Box stand at the 2004 Frieze Art Fair, London.

or representing things in order to appreciate, or at least understand, a different perspective, whether its a novel or a painting that's being read. It's this position that gives me the possibility of—in the case of the Frieze piece—attracting audience attention by stitching amendments to the otherwise familiar flags and thereby getting visitors to an art fair to catch themselves thinking about what they already know, but in relation to a context that isn't where they'd expect to think it. Therefore it's a different kind of reflection upon the subject. I'm juxtaposing things without ramming any message home. There's a useful neutral kind of a space generated between the experience of the art fair and the straightforward statistics embodied in the piece, back to that space for the viewer to inhabit between the source material and the physical outcome.

SO'R: Art is often talked about in terms of its capacity to communicate, yet, as Philip Roth points out, art deals with the nuance, while politics deals with generalities—in fact politics founders on instances of the nuance. Do you think that art can communicate politically despite this fundamental breach? Can the individuating tendency of art cope with the generalizing tendencies of politics?

GW: Thinking about how *International Trade Fair* fits into the frame you've just described ... the nuance you talk of is perhaps the quirk of the surprising or different means involved in the outcome, which is devised to deal with the generalities of the political in my recipe. (I'm trying to have my cake and eat it now!) Didn't Roth reflect aspects of himself through other characters in this sort of way, deploying a kind of literary ventriloquism? As I understand his approach, the books don't set out to solve life's problems, but rather to engage with them through the vehicle of a book, the structure of the tale, etc. He talks of using "what ifs" (what if Hitler hadn't lost?). I guess I'm proposing something along these lines, too, in terms of asking "so, what if we look at this another way?" Again, not offering solutions but simply raising issues. An example of this kind of approach, currently touring UK regional towns and presently in Rugby, where it's very much at home, is a work called *Interior Worlds* (Figures 2–5). This piece involves finding a number of empty, adjacent, plausibly domestic windows in the centre of various towns, above shops for example, and simply dressing them to look inhabited, but inhabited by an incredible diversity of individuals living cheek by jowl. The textiles I have been using are key to the effectiveness of this piece. There's not much between the reality they reflect and the fakery that is the work. Oh, and as much as possible, they are bought from charity shops in the area, partly so that at least some of the budget

Figure 2
Interior Worlds 2004 (Edinburgh).

Figure 3
Interior Worlds 2005 (Detail: Rugby).

Figure 4
Interior Worlds 2004 (Detail: Edinburgh).

goes to charity, but primarily because charity shops often contain chunks of the lives of real people: collections of used, worn, lived-with textiles and other stuff. I guess Mike Nelson constantly imports real-life material into his work in this way, but the major difference between this piece of mine and his approach is that he's making his work in and for art galleries. His works undermine our knowledge and expectations of those gallery buildings, but all along we know that it is fake. *Interior Worlds* is not shown in a gallery and therefore its edges blend into adjacent real life. Admittedly, there is a link connecting the work to a gallery and to the exhibition, *arttextiles 3*—the context that has brought it to town. A feature of this work perhaps worth mentioning is that, as much as possible, I've tried to make the piece visible from the

Figure 5
Interior Worlds 2005 (Detail: Artsway). Household fabrics and objects. Installation dimensions variable.

gallery using binoculars or a telescope. (Perhaps this line of sight performs like an umbilical cord, connecting the work to the white gallery space.)

Anyway, returning to your point: perhaps by embedding this piece out there in the everyday world in this way, proposing the opposite of a monumental public sculpture, the nuance that is the work engages with the generalities that are its surroundings and context. From this position it hopefully does have a plausible political voice.

SO'R: I can see how you might align this with a literary methodology: the recreation of observations, the synthesis of elements into a whole, selective reframing and so on. The main difference, however, is that reading a literary work takes a comparatively long time, whereas an artwork is more immediate in its totality. Can you talk about how you orchestrate the unfolding of these works, manipulate their readings in the absence of a timeline to lead the viewer by?

GW: The timeline resides in the actual unfolding of the work; as you suggest it does unfold like the reading of a text. However, perhaps this takes place after the initial encounter, or at least starting with that initial encounter with the work—if it's any good, that is! So therefore it takes place in the mind of the viewer. It's an individual experience, not unlike the reading of a text, but dependent upon ruminations around what's been consumed, observed, registered and retained. Rather than residing in a linear progression through a text, however, I hope the unfolding occurs more like a piece of downloaded compressed software (starting with what has been seen and remembered) "stuffit"-like, requiring unstuffing, unpacking. The work attempts ideally to deliver an initial framework that's easily grasped, but that then pulls the viewer along as it unpacks itself, or as it is spontaneously unpacked in the mind of the viewer. I guess this happens in different ways, according to the work in question. *Interior Worlds* relies a lot on the associations brought into play by what is suggested and inferred at each window, through associations personal to the viewer. *International Trade Fair*, on the other hand, requires the viewer to grasp the framework of the piece (statistics represented in graphic form) in order to travel from being simply bunting (its intended initial impact) towards the opening up of the political in relation to the context. Simon Patterson's *The Great Bear* is an example of a work that perhaps functions along similar lines: starting out as apparently familiar information (the London Underground map), it is soon transformed upon examination into a structure which sparks a train of thought (excuse the pun), touching upon historical progression, relationships between disciplines, individuals, time etc.

I'm now wondering just how typical the two examples of my work that we've raised so far are in these terms. I'm thinking of the rather ridiculously named *Umbria Cranberry Fold* (the first two words being the manufacturer's name for the fabric) made for an exhibition at medievalmodern a year or so ago (Figures 6 and 7). How does this fit in? It was made of a large quantity of deep-red, stage-curtain-like hanging cloth and was basically a scaled-up version of a medieval carved wooden "linenfold" panel, filling a whole wall of the gallery and shown alongside the actual medieval panel that was its reference point. The work attempted to make cloth do what linenfold (the carved representational device which refers to cloth) attempts to tell us that cloth does. But as a product of its scale and the specific fabric, it brought into play a variety of textile qualities and reference points (such as suggested function and extension of space, largely imported through haptic, acoustic and other sensory aspects of the cloth) that were absolutely not present in the wooden panel. So the straightforward reversal of a transposition was its starting point in terms of the reading of the work. It hopefully did unfold from that point, unpacking itself from that initial framework, as is the case with the Patterson piece, as well as *Interior Worlds* and *International Trade Fair*. Different subjects, different ranges of reference material, but yes, somehow these all appear to unpack in similar ways.

Figure 6
Medieval linenfold panel. Dimensions approx. 30 × 30 cm. The panel was used as the starting point for *Umbria Cranberry Fold* and was exhibited alongside the work shown in Figure 7.

Figure 7
Umbria Cranberry Fold 2004 (installation view). Dimensions approx. 360 × 300 cm. Fabric (former: plywood, metal, plastic).

SO'R: So the illusory fold is a literal, albeit *trompe-l'oeil*, prefiguring of the undulations of meaning in the viewers' imaginations. It would be too neat if this were your reasoning behind the use of textiles. I imagine, as you begin to suggest, that there are many other attributes of cloth that you employ in any one piece. I am thinking of the work of Berbardo Giorgi, who takes the perimeters of socially and historically important areas of Torino (for example, the area around the Fiat car factory, where immigrants established a community in the 1960s) and uses these as patterns for clothing, which are then made up by the Senegalese fashion designer Niass Mamadou. Giorgi likens the flux of social movements to the flow of fabric, which, if you stretch the metaphor, become distilled into garments—restrictive and concealing social indicators.

GW: Well no, the actual folded form and its relation to conceptual unfolding is not the reason behind my use of textiles here. That's not what I'd intended anyway! The shifting of one set of information (the map) from its status as information to become a component of an awkward garment in the Giorgi piece that you refer to is much more representative of the type of shift that went on in *Umbria Cranberry Fold*. I was interested in what was proposed by the wooden panel and how it attempted a representation of cloth, but one that was subject to the limitations of the material (timber) and the scale (ten inches square or so). I was drawn to the idea of attempting to build what was suggested because I knew it was going to be awkward and absurd, but also that it would highlight the fact that the carved panel is merely an evocative device and was not intended to be followed as some kind of a proposal. What happens when it is dealt with as a kind of proposal and is realized (and shown alongside the panel itself), is that we are led to reconsider the nature of the essentially decorative representation in the panel, but what we also start to examine and physically confront are the implications of what the panel actually suggests and how its realization affects both us and the architectural space (including the acoustics) in ways that go beyond our expectations. This happened largely through the specific nature of the fabric and its behavior in relation to both space and audience. It also caused us to reflect back upon the panel itself, thus changing it somehow by virtue of a context that it has generated for and by itself. The panel was not intended to be examined as one might examine an artwork, even in the terms that this would have taken place when it was made. I guess this kind of examination of material not intended to be examined in quite the way I'm choosing to examine or represent it is emerging as a bit of a habit!

SO'R: You might say that you are interested in translating from one format or material into an object or image that is illogical—a mapping from sense to nonsense. What this invariably does, however, is not demonstrate the absurdity of your work, but often the absurdity of the original information: the skewed statistics of galleries at Frieze, the oddness of folded cloth carved from wood, the placing of ornaments on a windowsill as a signifier of personality.

GW: Maybe not so clearly from "sense" to "nonsense". These terms seem like extremes that are too much polar opposites. Perhaps more like a translation, a transposing from one realm of sense to another, a process which then leads us to look back at the original or native sense as just that: the original context for the subject of my work, but the looking back takes place with the benefit of the experience of having seen the subject positioned elsewhere.

Mapping is a good word to use here; it illustrates the fact that there is some kind of new pathway established between the original sense and a new sense. The absurdity is an important element too. Our conventional ways of categorizing, looking at and evaluating aspects of our surroundings and the way we live are pretty absurd a lot of the time. It is this fact that I take as the excuse to be just as absurd myself with the buttoned-up statistics, etc., that can be my starting point. Absurdity introduces an element of fun into the proceedings. There's definitely an irreverent, tongue-in-cheek attitude going on in the work too, not to undermine the need to make a serious point, I intend that the serious content often benefits from a kind of sugar coating of absurdity in the delivery.

SO'R: You quite often work in series (there is a definite series of works that used decorative interior molding profiles, the four or five large floor-to-ceiling stretched fabric works, several pieces made in art shipping cases and the repetition and evolution of *Interior Worlds*, which we've talked of already). Often a multiplicity is a way of expressing variance, permutation and a potentially infinite number of riffs on a theme or idea. Your choice of domestic materials compounds this, as it references the infinite combinations of choices that people make—color, lavishness, period, level of decorativeness, etc—which build up into a portrayal of taste. Tell me about the dynamics of taste, choice and the series in your work.

GW: Taste very definitely comes into play in relation to the kind of portraiture involved in *Interior Worlds*, it's what is put to work to set one pseudo-individual expression off against the next. Adjacent incompatible expressions of taste begin to generate a kind of dynamic friction between one another. I guess this is a good example of the use of the absurd in the work. It's a kind of leveller; the different expressions of taste, people's choices, begin to look as absurd as one another, thereby perhaps causing us to reflect upon just how redundant these expressions are, including our own choices. At the same time, pointing out the absurdity through the juxtaposition of tastes leads to a kind of liberation, allowing us to acknowledge, celebrate and enjoy for the hell of it the ridiculousness of this kind of individual expression, including our own!

Working in series is something that I've chosen to do for a variety of reasons. As a tool it has definitely got something to do with enjoying what you describe as riffs: repeating, developing, shifting the emphasis upon and within a formula. Exploring the behavior of an idea in new circumstances (place, curatorial context, etc.) and indeed within the expanding context that a series generates for itself. One unique work is very different in isolation, as opposed to the same work forming part of a series. The concept of such a series of works was realized back in 1993. It borrowed the forms of standard timber moulding profiles (architraves, dados, picture frames) and used a range of equivalent white/off white brocade fabrics (Figure 8), equivalent native British hardwood veneers (oak, ash, beech etc) and British town names as titles

Figure 8
Chepstow, *Monmouth* and *York*
1993. Dimensions of largest work:
245 × 58 × 57 cm. All three works:
fabric and wood.

(Monmouth, York, Chepstow etc). These works are in fact compounds of equivalents, variations on a theme, riffs. An idea that uses a structure such as this could *only* work well as a series. The individual works somehow function more satisfactorily because they are a part of the group. In this case the basic idea or formula could be expanded in the mind of the viewer, once the viewer has grasped the rules and seen a few of the pieces, they could invent fictional additions to the series for themselves. Perhaps this structure helps reflect something interesting in relation to what you described in your question as the infinite combinations of choices that people make? When working on *Interior Worlds* in Rugby, I allowed the local students, who helped me remake the piece, to make choices and thereby change and expand the series of windows themselves. Once the basic framework was explained to them they spontaneously offered alternatives, questioning my choices, which helped to expand the series. There is some kind of democracy going on here, which also, I suppose, raises questions around authorship. This is definitely something I enjoy working with.

SO'R: So, with your tongue-in-cheek irreverence and invitation to the audience to extrapolate your work, you are being essentially generous. Unlike, say, film or television, where the narrative is apparent and generally fairly complete and little input is expected from the viewer, your work is open to much more subjective receptions. Again, it is more literary in this sense—the subjective experience of the individual reader/viewer is prioritized as well as the authorship, as opposed to the passive reception of a film, in which plot, narrative and esthetics are FIRMLY established. What becomes even more interesting, then, is when you incorporate historical or economical facts—I am thinking of the statistical pieces such as *International Trade Fair*—and things start to get rather self-reflexive. A gallerist may be walking around the art fair, see the piece and experience something approaching a pang of moral responsibility. Now, this might be rather optimistic, but it is a crucial parallel to literary theories of metafiction, where a novel that has a problematic relationship to history (i.e. it is not quite possible to extricate the "fact" from the "fiction") implicates the reader into history itself by making them decide what is "truth" and what is "fiction". Post-formalist work, which exists in the fabric of society rather than the autonomous gallery space, is like a contemporaneous version of this process: the viewer, by imaginatively adding to the work, starts having to consider the process of constructing such representations. In the case of *Interior Worlds*, the viewer becomes a sociologist, investigating stereotypes and visual culture.

GW: I agree with you about the way that film and television can deliver too much and leave no space for the viewer. In terms of my ideals (and being optimistic), you're spot on, thinking of *International Trade Fair*. Whether a dealer felt that pang or more probably just thought "there's an artist who wants me to feel a pang of guilt" is another matter. Still, more importantly and more realistically, the issue was raised, the invitation was made to the viewer (dealer or not) to reconsider their adopted position or role from within the context that made sense of that posture: the art fair itself. That's a self-reflexive process, you're right. Perhaps that's what was key in terms of the work's ambition: inviting individuals to reconsider their position as a participant at the event, not to take too much for granted, but to think more completely about their adopted role at the fair and the fair itself as a phenomena. If the pangs were felt too, then that's a bonus. Am I perhaps being over-optimistic in terms of my expectations of people in this kind of environment?

As for your idea of comparing the viewer of *Interior Worlds* relative to the position of a reader's relationship to a metafictional text, it's a very interesting take on the way that the work behaves. Metafiction covers a range of degrees in relation to fiction, if I understand correctly. I imagine we could draw parallels between these degrees of extremity and individual works of art as examples? I'm not sure how my work would fit in to this idea though.

SO'R: There are a number of levels at which metafictions deal with their own fictionality. There are those that deal with their status as fiction; in the context of art, you might think of the magical or utopianist painted landscapes that proliferate in galleries at the moment. They announce their divergence from mimetic representation but remain within the tradition of landscape painting. Then there is work that displays an ontological insecurity precisely by placing the contents of one structure within the framework of another, thereby interrogating its own fictionality on more than one level. Surrealism worked with this, inscribing psychoanalytical readings onto imagery. Then there is the work that is self-conscious to such an extent that it disappears up its own self-interrogation; it rejects realism to the point that it is immiscible with recognizable material conditions. Funnily enough, I can't think of any examples of this. Anyway, I think that your work is closest to the second model—it's aware of its own fiction and form.

GW: Yes, so the viewer has to negotiate the territory set out by the piece, navigate for themselves in that territory, in order to find a position somewhere between the sociological implications and content/of the work *and* the form that embodies this content *and* the place from which they are invited to consider all this (a regional town center, the Frieze art fair etc.). It's a landscape that they locate themselves within relative to these landmarks. This process involves making decisions and value judgments, which are a product of personal views, opinions and tastes. The viewer could be said to have to become, as you've suggested, a sociologist in *their* territory, investigating stereotypes and such-like, but thinking particularly in relation to the way they impact or mean something, or are read by themselves as individuals. All this talk makes the viewer's job sounds like a difficult one! Actually this process—the thinking, the navigating—is all something that should happen spontaneously as a part of the unstuffing, the natural process of the unpacking of the work, we talked of this earlier.

By suggesting that we look at particular works in various ways (e.g. in terms of the way that metafiction exists and is deployed in literature), you are, in a way, leading me and the readers of this text to reflect on the way the piece itself functions. You're helping us to understand my approach by inviting us to consider the work in relation to various parallel ideas that shed a different light on it—exactly what the work itself sets out to do in relation to its subject! If we extend the literary ideas that you've brought into play already, it's involved with the use of a kind of metaphor.

Taking this tack further, and returning to the analogy of compressed software, the term software perhaps first became implicated in post-formalist thinking relative to art through the art historian Jack Burnham. When software was a relatively new notion 1970, he curated the "Software" exhibition at the Jewish Museum in New York City. The subtitle was "Information Technology: Its New Meaning for Art." The exhibition used the new term "software" set against the old term "hardware" as a metaphor for what Burnham saw as the two components of art making: software as ideas, methods, thinking, concepts and hardware as (physical) outcomes, product. He defined "Post-Formalist Art" as meaning performance, interactive art and conceptual art as characterized by its concern with "software" as defined above. This idea also proposed the possibility of producing art without producing things, and that logically these outcomes should be staged in non-art situations, outside galleries. I'm not sure whether that little ramble shed any light on anything useful. Still, it serves to put a stick in the sand back there in 1970 relative to a few aspects of what we've been discussing!

Can I pick up on some of your earlier words? "...the viewer, by imaginatively adding to the work, starts having to consider the process of constructing such representations..." Moving on from this specific comment, can we consider an aspect of another work of mine, which involved a more direct public contribution to the development of the form that the work finally took? For a piece called *From The Outside Looking In* (Figure 9)

Figure 9
From The Outside Looking In 1996. Dimensions 360 × 340 × 330 cm. Fabric, plywood and metal.

I asked the good folk of the town of Munster in Germany to draw from memory the shape of a very distinctive line from the map of their town. It's the remnant of a not-quite-complete star-shaped moat around the historic seat of power. This line is like a crude child's drawing, somehow at odds with the rest of the map—bold and totally memorable. The resultant set of drawings, made by the burgers of Munster were overlaid by computer to produce an average line. This line was then scaled up, drawn onto the gallery floor, projected from floor to ceiling and used as profiles between which to stretch fabric, producing a room-sized, sound-dampened, new interior space in the warehouse-like gallery. The cloth connected the audience nicely to notions of grand comfortable interior space, even verging on the theatrical. What was interesting about the drawing process was the clear democracy of both the process and the resulting line. However, while this approach somehow logically reflects the view of a large number of people, in terms of how the line appears to them, what was actually produced was a long way from the "truth". It was simultaneously the truth and not the truth. I'm leaving the viewer to take a view (position) again aren't I?

SO'R: It is a perennial problem within liberal democracies to balance consensus with marginalia and here you demonstrate that, en masse, people fluctuate from one another dramatically and this sets up complex flows of influence. I have a vague memory of something I heard on the radio, when a social scientist described an experiment in which a group of people gave individual answers to a question, which were then analyzed en masse. The group's average response was more likely to be correct than if a random individual were asked the question and the scientist suggested that it is better to travel in packs after all. It's a knotty problem, the relationship between the one and the many, and something that the artist must face continually, shifting from the studio to the gallery, the multitude of subjects to the singular art object, your intention to the viewers' interpretations. I guess the upshot is that, in the realm of perception, there is no ultimate control.

Resistance and Submission, Warp and Weft: Unraveling the Life of Ethel Mairet

Abstract

This paper attempts to unravel some of the knots of handweaver Ethel Mairet's biography, and to embrace the paradoxes, political vagaries, and textures of her life. At once appropriator and colonizer, Indian nationalist and Sri Lankan scholar, twice married, twice divorced, feminist, submissive wife, communist sympathizer, businesswoman and feminized weaver, Ethel Mairet complicated virtually every trope of "feminine," "craft," and "colonial"—both within her life, and in attempts to write her into history. This paper examines Mairet's complicated relationships to these categories, and her negotiation of the roles prescribed for her through, in the appropriate words of artist and art historian Mireille Perron: "resistance and submission, warp and weft."

KIRSTY ROBERTSON
Kirsty Robertson is a PhD candidate in the Department of Art at Queen's University in Kingston, Canada. Her recent work examines the visual culture of the global justice movement and the use and circulation of textiles in contemporary activism and globalization. Her work has been widely published in journals such as Public (Canada), *The Journal of American and Comparative Cultures*, and catalogues such as *Image and Imagination* (2005).

Resistance and Submission, Warp and Weft: Unraveling the Life of Ethel Mairet

"Women can drop out of the already fragile history of the crafts with alarming ease," writes Tanya Harrod in her survey of the crafts in Britain in the twentieth century (Harrod 1999: 118). And while this is indeed the case, the corollary might be that those who are remembered, those few whose lives and careers are archived against erasure, run the risk of being pulled into a narrative that smoothes edges and purges the idiosyncratic in an effort to create this initial history of women in the crafts. Take, for example, the life of the British handweaver Ethel Mairet, remembered through a monograph and exhibition catalogue on her life and work, an online archive put together by the Crafts Study Centre in Surrey, England, and a number of passing references in more recent histories of British Arts and Crafts (Figure 1).[1] But this paper is still, in the first instance, an act of reclamation, one that I will argue is made necessary by the fact that Mairet's life and work resist easy categorization.[2] At once appropriator and colonizer, Indian nationalist and Sri Lankan scholar, twice married, twice divorced, feminist, submissive wife, Communist sympathizer, businesswoman and feminized weaver, Ethel Mairet complicates virtually every trope of "feminine," "craft," and "colonial"—both within her life, and in attempts to write her into history. What results then, is a double fate: either the simplification of her problematic relationships to these categories, or her erasure from mainstream written history.

This paper is an attempt to unravel some of the knots of Mairet's biography, and to embrace the paradoxes, political vagaries, and textures of her life. What might we learn from Mairet, and the complications of her life that have been recorded and remembered (or forgotten)? How do Mairet's life and work speak to the performance of gender and social roles, both within early twentieth-century Britain, and also within the art historical practices that follow several decades of feminist and post-colonial re-writings of canonical scripts? Could it be that even the most open of systems, when set within the disciplinary structure of art history, continue to maintain boundaries of categorization that refuse contradiction and erase ambiguity? If so, then Mairet's life within this system is a round peg in a square hole, negotiating the roles prescribed for her through, in the appropriate words of artist and art historian Mireille Perron: "resistance and submission, warp and weft" (Perron 1998: 124).

An enigma to be sure, as she worked to revive the British handweaving industry, Mairet

Figure 1
Ethel Mairet weaving, 1930s.
Collection Crafts Study Centre Part
of Series: One of three. Current
Accession Number 2002.21.16

produced hundreds of textiles using combinations of woolen and artificial materials, geometric and appropriated design, and hand-mixed vegetable dyes (Figure 2). Her work was of profound importance to textile production of the early to mid-twentieth century, influencing not only British design, but also the Indian handweaving and independence movements, while also paving the way for the simple lines of designers such as Coco Chanel in the 1930s. By the mid 1930s, she was considered one of the most important craftworkers in Britain, and was singled out by the potter Bernard Leach as an artist who had left behind the legacy of William Morris to give the British craft scene "a new life during the last twenty years" (Harrod 1999: 9).

Born Ethel Mary Partridge in Barnstaple, England, in 1872, Mairet was quickly introduced to the Arts and Crafts movement through her brother Fred Partridge, whose links to the local arts community offered Mairet an alternative to the traditional options open to young middle-class women. Barnstaple, on the north Devon coast, was home to a number of Arts and Crafts practitioners, including architect and designer W. R. Lethaby, who introduced Partridge to Guild of Handicraft founder C. R. Ashbee, beginning a family friendship with the Ashbees that would continue through Mairet's life (Coatts 1983:

Figure 2
Ethel Mairet at a Red Rose Guild exhibition, 1930s. Rights managed by the Crafts Study Centre.

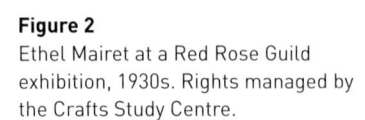

11–12.)[3] In 1902, after a stint as a governess, Mairet met Ananda Coomaraswamy, a "brilliant Anglo-Ceylonese biologist," and quickly married him before heading off on a series of trips to Sri Lanka and India (Coatts 1983: 14).[4] While there, Mairet learned how to weave, in between accompanying Coomaraswamy on a number of trips to collect artifacts that would eventually form the basis of the Indian art collection at the Boston Museum of Fine Arts (Coatts 1983: 23; Figure 3). When her marriage broke up in 1910, she returned to England and began weaving professionally, setting up a series of workshops, and marrying the much younger Philip Mairet not long after. She soon moved to The Gospels in Ditchling, which was to become her home and main site of business, staying there after their divorce (Sisson 1981: 50–70).

Figure 3
Ethel Mairet at an upright loom, 1950s. Rights managed by the Crafts Study Centre.

Ethel Mairet fits neither into a patriarchal nor a feminist art history; she stands out neither in the category of New Woman nor of the conservative middle-class lady, and like all weavers, is generally erased from traditional art historical narratives that privilege the arts over the crafts. In part, this is because it is difficult to set up the sort of progressive evolution from artifact to artifact that is possible in the traditional history of Western art, but also because craft production is often associated with the domestic and material space, far removed from the world of art. But if, as Judith Butler suggests, all such categories are instruments of regulatory regimes, setting up systems of normalization (women's art, for example), that exclude even as they work for inclusivity, perhaps it is Mairet's slippages between categories that might interest us here (Butler 1991: 13–14).

This is not, then an attempt to define the difference or sameness of Mairet from her contemporaries, but to the unearth some of the processes of identification and differentiation, primarily through gender, but also through race, by which Mairet has been doubly written out of the archive (Moore 1993: 2). While taking into account that to write in this way might simply enable the formation of new categories, Mairet's disruption of boundaries, even when situated within her own relatively privileged upbringing and heterosexual relations, offers a rich account of the multiplicity of directions that the repetitive performance (and failure of that performance) of gender and race might take (Butler 1991: 16).

In analyzing how Mairet constructed herself under, and was constructed by, a patriarchal society, it is difficult to separate fact from projection, as the extremes of Mairet's admittedly volatile personality are often heightened or obscured depending on the purpose of the account. In 1952, her obituary in the London Times read:

> *Surrounded by her textiles, which she had made or collected from many lands, and with successive families of Siamese cats and kittens, [Ethel Mairet] was an unforgettable figure, spare and energetic and with a zest for life and work that carried her through times of loneliness and frustration to fresh efforts and new friendships. (London Times, November 26, 1952)*

While the picture of a lonely woman surrounded by cats is not entirely flattering, neither is her eccentricity so unusual that the extremes cannot also be easily flattened to reconstitute Mairet into descriptions of the feminine. Though experimental in her weaving techniques, for example, Mairet's love life appears to have been resolutely heterosexual and monogamous, allowing her to slide smoothly into a tradition of mythical waiting weavers, such as the Lady of Shalott, Penelope and Mariana. Within the context of a 1980s feminist project to reclaim forgotten women artists then, in the 1983 retrospective of her work, Ethel Mairet is championed as the reviver of the tradition of modern handweaving in England, but is also described as a woman with an "intuitive appreciation of color," who is credited with not descending into "arty crafty" or "precious" work (Coatts 1983: 9).

According to art historian Cheryl Buckley, even though female textile artists transform nature into culture through the design process, they are always already associated with nature, and are tied to their biology through a patriarchal ideology that defines their design skills as a product of their sex—as natural or innate, instinctive and emotional (Buckley 1989: 253). In virtually all of the limited post-1980 writing concerning her work, Mairet's business acumen is subsumed to such descriptions, writing, in effect, a celebration of women's creativity that creates what Jill Seddon calls a "pseudo-inclusion," trapping even as it reclaims (Seddon 2000: 427). Take, for example, Christopher Frayling of the Royal College of Art who, sifting through the numerous descriptions of Mairet, chose to quote a decontextualized snippet from Mairet's friend Janet Ashbee, stating that Mairet had "an intelligence rather of feeling than of brain" (quoted in Coatts 1983: 10). A 1987 response to an exhibition of her work noted "her emphasis on the intuitive and hand-crafted aspect made her for a longtime shun technology" (James 1987: 60), while in 1984, art historian Alan Crawford wrote of Mairet that "her instincts were simple ... [and] pattern and structure ... were, in a sense beyond her."[5]

Figure 4
Three handwoven scarves in various wools, 1938–45, 1933–5, 1945–50 (left to right in the image). Rights managed by the Crafts Study Centre.

Crawford's comments seem a bit injudicious, given that a brief examination of Mairet's work shows a good knowledge of pattern and experimentation—and an excellent understanding of the procedural quality of pattern built up (structured) through the warp and weft of weaving (Figures 4 and 5). In fact, given that weaving can be described as a sort of soft engineering, with its system of warp and weft comparable to the binary code of modern computer programming, there seems little doubt that the characterization of Mairet's weaving as largely instinctive and emotional is based on the sort of gender exclusion outlined by Buckley. After the 1983 exhibition of Mairet's work that was supposed to, as Crawford wrote in the same article "put Ethel Mairet firmly on the map" (Crawford 1984: 46), Mairet was instead moved to a map of another sort—one situating women firmly in a sphere of intuitive and instinctual response, undoing the act of reclamation even as it was in process. For the most part, the brief flurry of activity surrounding the 1983 publication of craft historian Margot Coatts's remarkably detailed account of Mairet's life and work is reducible to a few brief words: "instinct," "feeling," and "intuition."

Interestingly, this is not the case with pre-1950 interpretations of Mairet's life and work. A contemporary text from the 1946 *Architecture Review* makes no mention of Mairet's "instinctive" appreciation of color, nor of her "intuitive" approach to weaving, concentrating instead on her argument for the need for hand-design in a machine society: "We respect [the words of Ethel Mairet] because we know that Mrs. Mairet turns to hand weaving not for the purpose of machine boycott but for the sake of machine mastery," write the (primarily male) members of the Advisory Committee on Design, and authors of the article.

Figure 5
Handwoven length of tartan (plain weave, cotton and wool), 1940s. Warp: stripes of varying width in yellow, red, bottle green and black cotton; weft: repeat stripes of brown, red and green wool. Twenty ends per inch, twenty picks per inch. Rights managed by the Crafts Study Centre.

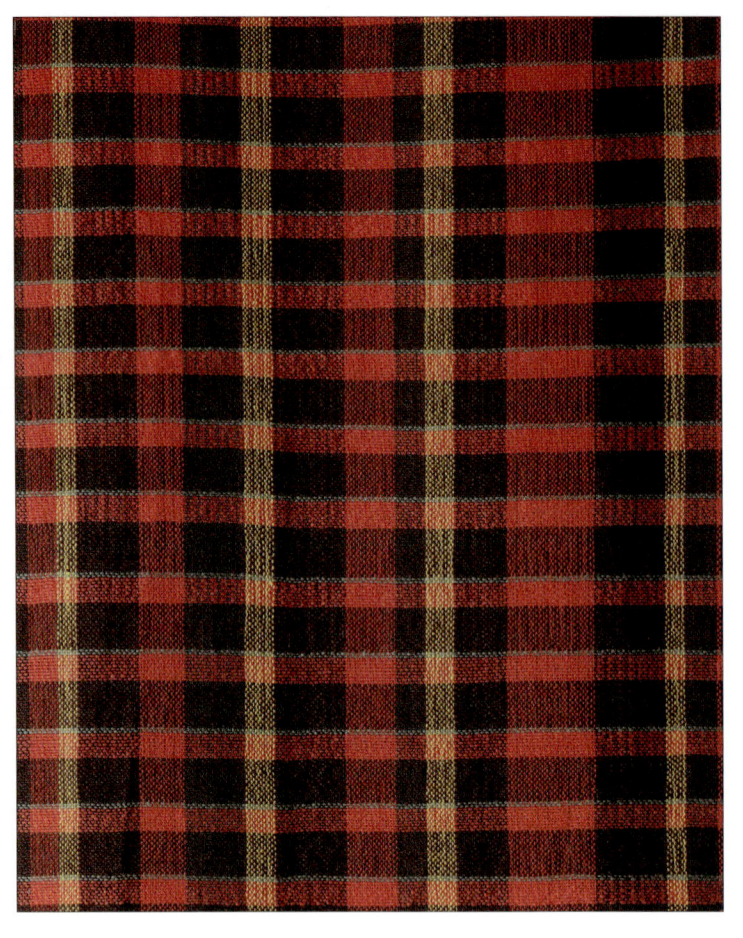

The text continues: "It is harder to become a well-trained weaver than a well-trained metal or leather worker or a printer," noting that "[weaving] is far from just throwing a shuttle." The authors then note Mairet's "scientific" knowledge of dyeing, her understanding of mass production, and conclude with the words:

and we can at least visualize an industry geared up for high rates of production, but whose products are constantly guided, developed and enriched by highly sensitive designers working out their experiments on the hand-loom. Already this is taking place and we take the opportunity of giving it what support we can by these notes and the accompanying illustrations. (Advisory Committee 1946: 91)

What to make of the gap between the pre-1950 and post-1980 interpretations of Mairet's work? In writing and in practice, Mairet had no problem complicating the notion of weaving as domestic craft. Returning in 1907 from five years in Sri

Figure 6
Ethel Coomaraswamy weaving at Norman Chapel, 1910s. Rights managed by the Crafts Study Centre.

Lanka, Mairet promptly turned the domestic home into her workspace, and progressively into a site of business. Her home, Norman Chapel, in Broad Campden in the Cotswolds, and now an icon of British Arts and Crafts architecture and design, was built in her absence, and when she returned she quickly pushed the specially carved piano into the corner, placing her loom at the centre of the living space where it was tripped over, cursed, but always present (Figure 6). Following her second divorce and the formation of her successful workshop, The Gospels, which produced fabrics for clothing and sale, Mairet was living in her business rather than weaving in her home.

However, this is not to suggest a utopian element to Mairet's life, for it might have been precisely her lack of threat to the system that allowed her the freedom to weave for profit and to be characterized as a successful businesswoman. In fact, Mairet's loom literally loomed over her personal life, and the time she did not spend weaving was spent desperately trying to save her two failing marriages, consistently underestimating her intelligence in a male presence, and urgently trying to conceive a child in order to preserve her marriage to her first husband. Her production of textiles for profit at the expense of her production of children was a constant threat to the imaginary life constructed for her by society. So too was her interracial marriage, her numerous trips to Sri Lanka and India, and her burgeoning interest in the Indian independence movement.

Because of her first husband, the now revered art historian and philosopher Ananda Coomaraswamy, Mairet became both a cultural appropriator and an Indian nationalist—the two, in her mind, working together, but sitting uncomfortably at the juncture of recent feminist and post-colonial scholarship. In 1903 the Coomaraswamys traveled to Sri Lanka, ostensibly for a geographic survey of which Ananda was the head. Coomaraswamy, who had been in England since childhood, was shocked by what he saw as the decadence of middle-class Sri Lankan society.[6] Like so many writers in the British Arts and Crafts *Studio Magazine*, he felt that the culture of India and Sri Lanka was suffering and degenerating as a result of the introduction of European machinery and the consequent production of hybrid works of art. He thus felt that Sri Lankan society should look to its pre-colonial past to reinvigorate itself. Mairet shared many of Coomaraswamy's ideas, developing what for the time can be seen as an anti-racist and anti-imperialist position. She wrote to Janet Ashbee:

I am glad that you have seen something of the Anglo-Saxon in contact with color and you can perhaps understand something of the hatred it stirs up in me when I come across it ... A culture that is not of the West is no culture in the eyes of the majority, How impossibly unsympathetic and unimaginative it all is. (quoted in Coatts 1983: 32)[7]

On the 1903 trip Mairet insisted on recording the arts and crafts of each village, taking extensive notes and visiting museums and private collections. What she saw led her to believe even more strongly that the culture of Sri Lanka was being destroyed by imperialism. Mairet, like Coomaraswamy, believed that "the character of steady competence which once distinguished the Kandyan craftsman has gone forever; a change such as the industrial revolution has brought about almost all over the world" (quoted in Coatts 1983: 16). Mairet's words, coming from a position of privilege, speak at once to her anti-imperial stance, and to her ignorance of, and patronizing attitude toward cultural issues outside of her own sphere.[8] The rhetoric of racial difference and colonial imperative, so prevalent in British society at this time, circles around Mairet, occasionally coming out in her own indifference towards exploitation in Africa—"it may require years of effort to grow sufficient cotton in the Congo to supply our needs..." she wrote in a 1939 text (Mairet 1939: 44). The same ambivalence is also present in reviews of her work. The British design critic Amelia Defries, exemplifying a temporal hierarchy that places so-called "primitive" cultures at the base of an evolutionary game of catch-up, wrote in a 1924 review:

> The problem confronting the modern craftsman is to get back to this true outlook [of "primitive" culture]... The coarse weaving by Mrs. Mairet, who delights in savage design, is not equal to the races she copies, but it is good strong work. (Defries 1924: 261–69)

Performative roles, however, are never fully contained, and for both Ethel Mairet and Ananda Coomaraswamy, the roles of colonizer/colonized, whether through race or gender, were multifaceted. According to textile historian Margot Coatts, when Mairet and Coomaraswamy married, they met with some prejudice from both the Indian and British communities, though their marriage was "admired" by their friends (Coatts 1983: 12). Coatts's choice of the word "admired" is interesting, for in much of the correspondence surrounding both this marriage, and Mairet's later marriage to Philip Mairet, a man fifteen years her junior, the word "admired" is used to cover inherent prejudice aimed at both Mairet and her husbands. Descriptions of Coomaraswamy from Mairet's friends, for example, are often prefaced by racial and racist markers such as "dark," "mysterious," "aloof," and "strange" (Crawford: 46). Janet Ashbee was certain she could "trace shreds of polygamous ancestry," that made her "shiver and draw back" (quoted in Coatts 1983: 30).

In spite of such comments, it was Coomaraswamy who was better able to negotiate these prescribed roles. Educated in England, intelligent, erudite, and sporting a markedly aristocratic figure and presence, it is Coomaraswamy who is given the role of "saving" Sinhalese art for posterity, resulting in several manuscripts, numerous biographies, a position at the Boston Museum of Fine Arts, and a mention in well-known author Michael Ondaatje's latest novel *Anil's Ghost*. The great tome *Medieval Sinhalese Art*, one of the few books on the topic, was dedicated to Ethel Mairet (through her initials only), but the writing, research and photography that she did for the work remains unmarked outside of Coomaraswamy's introduction (Coomaraswamy 1956). It has also been forgotten that Coomaraswamy, who retired as an amazingly well-read and prolific art historian, had little interest in Sinhalese art (he did, after all, travel to Sri Lanka

Figure 7
Handwoven samples showing vegetable dying techniques and the influence of Indian weaving techniques, 1920–25. The samples were originally part of Ethel Mairet's sample book, but were remounted for the exhibition "A weaver's life. Ethel Mairet 1872–1952," Crafts Study Centre, Bath, 25 August–30 October 1983, and tour. Rights managed by the Crafts Study Centre.

to study its geology), before Mairet encouraged him to engage with it.

Given to occupying the spaces between cultures, between gender roles and between classes, it might not be surprising that Mairet's weaving is rarely a wholesale adoption of design, but more often a hybrid of technique and style. Unlike other British Arts and Crafts artists, such as ceramicist William de Morgan, Mairet never appropriated complete designs, writing "[e]ach country has its own expression, and it is rare, or practically impossible that good results can be obtained by copying one another" (Mairet 1929: 14). However, the influence of her trips to Sri Lanka, as well as later trips to Yugoslavia and Scandinavia to view peasant weaving, is palpable in her own textiles (Figure 7). The geometric style and bright color of her early work is a hybrid of Indian colors and patterns and British techniques. The texture she added to the later fabric she created, and the combination of hand-woven materials with man-made ones such as rayon and cellophane, were a second concession to a hybridization of the hand-made with the male order of machine-woven textiles.[9]

What Mairet criticized in the work of the Kandyan craftsmen when she was learning how to weave was what showed up in her own later working through of the juxtaposition between the hand-made and the industrial. Rosalind Krauss presents a somewhat different reading of appropriation and the hybrid that is useful in this context. According to Krauss, the hybrid (both those produced by the colonized under European influence, and those produced in Europe with influence from the colonies) "overcomes and undermines gender inscriptions of existing cultural languages, particularly those enmeshed within the discourses of modernism" (Krauss 1986: 196). The patriarchal language of modern art is challenged by hybrid forms that replace, quote, parody, contaminate and are contaminated by "Other" languages and gender inscriptions, thereby undermining the dominant language of art (Krauss 1986: 151–71). According to Krauss's analysis, to produce weavings containing influence from Sri Lanka as well as combining modern and traditional materials and methods of fabric production, is to doubly undermine a male domination of the art canon. What it does to the privilege of colonial relations is somewhat less clear, particularly as Mairet's appropriation came at the expense of her accepting change in Kandyan techniques of weaving.

As it turns out, however, Mairet's knowledge of the various Indian and Sri Lankan weaving techniques led Mahatma Gandhi to seek her advice during his organization of a revival of Indian weaving traditions (Coatts 1983: 115; Singham 1974: 300–350). In this encounter, Mairet's textiles might be read as a formalization of the ideas behind Homi Bhabha's notion of third space, or the space of overlap in between cultures, and though translated through the politics of appropriation, in this context her textiles can be seen to have a latent political potential (Bhabha 1994). Like the Coomaraswamys, Gandhi had observed the destruction of traditional arts in India, but rather than taking the position that industrial revolution necessarily led to a decadent abandonment of traditional work, Gandhi emphasized the British role in the economic destruction of the Indian textile industry. In Gandhi's interpretation, wealth from India was taken by English businessmen, and spent primarily in England rather than circulating back into the Indian economy, thereby producing poverty and famine while destroying traditional economies. These problems were then exacerbated by low tariffs on British yarn and cotton coming into India and high tariffs on Indian textiles being exported. Indian craft workers were forced to produce hybrids in order to survive, while traditional crafts were forgotten (Bean 1989: 355–57).

As Sarat Maharaj points out, Gandhi's project involved the "de-feminization" of the textile trade. When spinning became a method of making large segments of the population self-sufficient it became a method of peaceful rebellion, rather than one of subordination. As Maharaj writes, Gandhi sought to move weaving into a space where it was sexually indifferent, where it became an "unmotivated sign system," akin to listening to music (Maharaj 1998: 182). Like Coomaraswamy, Gandhi advocated a sort of inverted Marxism, a "post-industrialism" that was anti-machinery, anti-capitalist, but also set against Marxism in its anti-industrial stance (Brantlinger 1996: 480). While I am not suggesting that Mairet played a large role in the Indian independence movement (she in fact moved away from the stance of post-industrialism), the now forgotten relationship between Gandhi and Mairet adds a further complication to any simple narrative of Mairet's weaving practice, complicating the easy interpretation that Mairet's appropriation of design, and benignly patronizing attitude, were simply fetishistic contextualizations and appropriations of "the other."

Mairet's support of the Indian independence movement was not her only foray into politics. Never a leader, but always politically engaged, she wrote in November 1908 that she was going to Manchester, Birmingham and Bristol with the suffragettes—at the time she was friends with Margaret Harwood, a suffragette organizer (Coatts 1983: 31). Around the same time she began writing on dress reform, calling for a style of dress that abandoned corsets for lighter, freer and more useful attire, made attractive through the use of embroidery techniques borrowed from India and China (Coatts 1983: 19). Describing Mairet in the days after her separation from Coomaraswamy, Janet Ashbee reported to her husband that "[s]he has been doing a lot of reading and going for a good deal of 'advanced' feminist literature" (quoted in Coatts 1983: 39).

Mairet's political engagement continued throughout her life. In 1937 she wrote to her friend and fellow weaver Marianne Straub of the situation in Europe. Setting her letter within a recommendation to read artist Moholy Nagy's new book, Mairet advocated his vision:

What a real communism it all is and how inevitable—even in the Fascist states. I feel the democratic states are keeping it back more than anything. And yet how it creeps in bit by bit—even in England—under a different name of course! (Mairet 1937)[10]

Her disappointment at the outbreak of war two years later was palpable, and turned to depression when she was hurt and part of her home destroyed during a bombing raid, before turning to a joy at being alive. In May 1941 she wrote to Coomaraswamy:

In these days we all live from day to day ... but it is the most exhilarating life experience and I am glad I wasn't killed last summer, one gets a creative reaction to the terrific destruction ... It is all so much better than the last war and we really are all in it now. (Mairet 1941)[11]

A class-consciousness that had been building for some time came to the fore during the war years, and throughout Mairet continued to advocate a communal (if not communist) style of living, criticizing her bourgeois students. "Olive is irritatingly selfish," she wrote in 1940, "she comes from the kind of bourgeois family I dislike (and every member of the family with a car and has no thought of helping anyone by it. She has her car here but only uses it for herself),"[12] while celebrating any actions that might break down class barriers:

> *I am thrilled about the air training scheme for young boys. I believe it to be one of the greatest moves forward that has happened yet. It will break down class feeling, it will make it possible for all to fly later as a matter of course, and it will educate all impartially. (Mairet 1941)*[13]

Mairet, like many of her colleagues, looked to Russia as a great hope, feeling that contact through the war could only have a positive effect on Britain. In a 1941 letter to Straub, she wrote "There is a glimmer of a beginning and I think it will come fast once it begins. Our contact with Russia will do a lot. But the hatred of Russia is still very deep."[14] For the most part, Mairet's politics, particularly her engagement with communism, are erased from written accounts of her work. In fact, her ideological stance, which she often thought through in terms of her weaving, was unusual for the time. As Tanya Harrod writes:

> *The male writers in the craft world attempted to construct intellectual systems which would accommodate their practice, as if the activity of craft on its own undermined their masculinity. This was hardly an issue for the women whose involvement in the crafts was rarely challenged. (Harrod 1999: 118)*

But Mairet did challenge the broader nature of craft production and society, engaging with politics, publishing the ideologically charged *Hand-Weaving Today* in 1939, and creating a homosocial environment within The Gospels— "I hate men in the workshop," she told the unfortunate Peter Collingwood when he came to work for her (Collingwood 1983: 22). She wrote to him proudly just before her death: "This is a critical workshop you know—more critical than any I have yet come across."[15]

But these comments were far in the future in 1910 when Mairet spent the summer experimenting with weaving, and then traveling with Coomaraswamy through India to collect works of art for the Indian Society of Oriental Art's United Provinces Exhibition, held in Allahabad in the winter of 1910–11. Mairet spent much of the trip collecting fabrics and noting the excitement of the bazaars. She returned home alone in 1911, her marriage to Ananda having broken up. Coomaraswamy had fallen in love with Alice Richardson, an art school friend of Philip Mairet, who would become Ethel Mairet's second husband (Coatts 1983: 36). The period was an incredibly difficult one for her. She wrote to Ashbee, "I can't live in Camden without Ananda, and I can't live in London because it's such hell, but what am I to do? My brain does not seem capable of conceiving a future. What an aimless individual is a woman without a cause" (quoted in Coatts 1983: 37). Not only did she have to work through what she saw as a betrayal by her husband and one of her friends, but she also had to clean out her beloved Norman Chapel and pack everything up.[16] She was 38 years old, with little income, no husband, and a belief that she had been left

Figure 8
Handwoven textile, late 1930s. The samples were originally part of Ethel Mairet's sample book, but were remounted for the exhibition "A weaver's life. Ethel Mairet 1872–1952," Crafts Study Centre, Bath, 25 August–30 October 1983, and tour. Rights managed by the Crafts Study Centre.

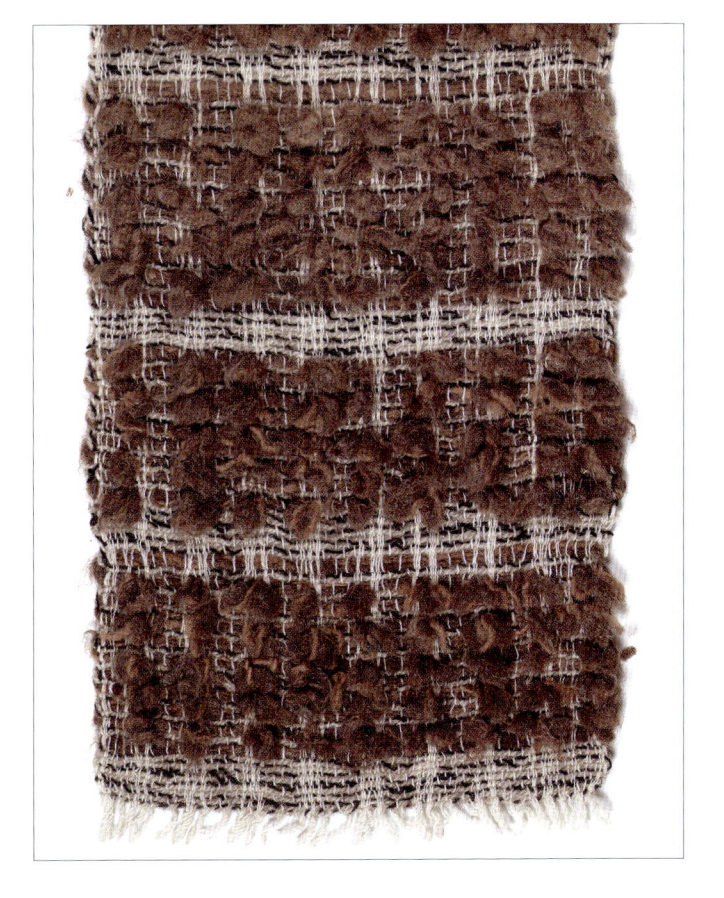

because she could not produce a child (Sisson 1981: 53).

Philip Mairet helped her clean out Norman Chapel, and to move into her own bungalow at Saunton Sands, which she had designed herself, but which was paid for by Coomaraswamy (Coatts 1983: 38). Despite their difficult separation, the two stayed in touch, with Coomaraswamy supporting Mairet until The Gospels became profitable. Because of this Mairet was able to find the funds to leave Saunton Sands to move to the Thatched House in Shottery, near Stratford-on-Avon, where she set up her first weaving workshop, and to her thinking, became a "woman with a cause."

Shortly after, Ethel and Philip Mairet were married—she was 42, he was 27. The marriage was not looked upon favorably by anyone, including Mairet's closest friends. The union was an unusual one, not only because of the difference in age, but also because the Mairets wrote their own marriage contract, designed to be renewed every ten years (Sisson 1981: 71–72).[17] In Philip Mairet's autobiography, he looks back on these years as an exciting time, though he constructs their marriage as a mistake. He frequently cites their difference in age, and in spite of his own infidelities, regrets the fact that her previous marriage was over, but the divorce not final when they met (Sisson 1981: 54). Describing a visit from Ethel he notes "I was faintly startled to note that her face looked rather older than I had remembered, nor had I seen the serious, intent and eager expression it now wore" (Ibid.). Nevertheless, in 1917 Ethel and Philip Mairet moved to The Gospels in Ditchling, an artists' community which was to become the main location for Mairet's weaving.[18] She had felt it necessary to leave Shottery after finding her sister-in-law had committed suicide in the weaving room by hanging (Coatts 1983: 47).[19] Further, the First World War was underway, and at Ditchling, Philip Mairet was able to work the land as a conscientious objector, though he was jailed before the war's end (Coatts 1983; 46–48).

At this time, Mairet began to concentrate almost entirely on weaving. In this she was something of a pioneer for, aside from a few outposts in Ireland, Wales and the Outer Hebrides (the home of Harris tweed), there was very little handweaving in the British Isles. The weavings produced by the Ditchling workshop generally used color in all-over stripes or patterned borders, often with the emphasis on texture or original mixes of materials (Figure 8). One reviewer wrote: "Her weaves were basic in concept—gauze (leno), hopsack, honeycomb or spaced threads—but absolutely new and fresh in her interpretation of them in terms of color, interest of yarns, and originality of thread arrangement" (Waller: 78). The clothing made by the workshop was, as Coatts described, "highly regarded among the cognoscente and seen as faintly unclean by the rest" (Coatts 1983: 83). Because of this, until the late 1930s, Mairet's designs were largely outside of typical fashion. The style of the time was modern, anti-Morris, and anti-Classic—according to contemporary art historian Antony

Hunt, buyers were "off birds and honeysuckle" (Hunt 1937: 20). Elegant, which Mairet's work was not, was in fashion, as were pale and bland colors, including beige, white, off-white and brown (Hunt 1937: 25).

In spite of being out of fashion (she deplored the use of bland browns), Mairet's weaving workshop prospered throughout the First World War and the Depression. It was also at this time that The Gospels began to receive a significant amount of interest. In an article titled "Mrs. Mairet's weaving industry" as part of a series on Women's Successful Enterprise in *The Queen* in 1932, Florence B. Low describes The Gospels as a welcoming, bustling, but relaxing place: "A girl was spinning at the wheel and another was weaving on the loom, both movements very graceful and pleasant to watch" (Low 1932: 35).[20] Set between articles telling Depression-era readers to use more "calves' heads, sheeps' heads, tripe, [and] beef collops" to make a budget go further, and articles on how to get one's hands clean if forced to work with dirty machinery in the factory, The Gospels does come across as a utopian space (Low 1932).[21] The author interviews Mairet, garnering her opinions on the need for "good taste" to assure the use of the "best and most artistic colors" when dyeing, on the effort to build up a "real English tradition" (but one that could "benefit from the techniques of other countries") and on Mairet's struggle to set up a successful enterprise (Low 1932: 35). Here Mairet is given the chance to construct herself as she wishes to be seen, and she loses no time in doing so: "It is not sufficient to be artistic and a good craftswoman," she says, "it is necessary to have a good head for business and to follow the trend of what the public wants" (Ibid.). She continues that women wanting to set up their own businesses should choose appropriate locales "somewhere near a motor road or in a pretty village which people visit, or in a good position in town" (Ibid.). Her points echo those of Ray Strachey, whose book *Careers and Openings for Women* (1935) suggested professions such as architect or craftworker, but cautioned:

> there are far more workers than there is work, and ... if a girl has to live upon her earnings a really high degree of talent must be combined with industry and perseverance and the skill to market her wares. (Strachey 1935: 187, quoted in Seddon 2000: 430)

It was also around this time that Mairet began to publish her own work in an effort to communicate her ideas on dyeing and weaving. In her writing she criticizes the use of chemical aniline dyes and "the recent fashion for muddy art colors" (Coomaraswamy 1916; Coatts 1983: 42–43). Following on William Morris's belief that aniline dyes were inferior to natural ones and little more than a capitalist ploy to gain profit at the expense of quality, Mairet refused to use them (Parry 1983: 39). Mairet was willing to delve further into industrial capitalism than Morris had been, using synthetic yarns and suggesting that the machine was necessary to textile production, though all design and form should be controlled by the human hand (Coatts 1983: 82). She wrote "the reform[er] does not develop a machine boycott, but a machine mastery" (Mairet 1939: 11–12). Perhaps closer to the purpose of the Bauhaus than the British Arts and Crafts movement, she came to believe that the machine should not be seen as a money maker but a means "for the better ordering of life, easing hard and laborious work, making for the appreciation of beauty in city, village and home" (Ibid.). Mairet came to see the essential flaw of Morris's work in the disastrous effect of isolating individual craftsmen, separating them from industry. "We are still suffering from the William Morris tradition," she wrote to a friend, "that immense struggle of individualist craftsmen to combat the hell of the machine that we had then got into."[22] Permanently outside of society because of his (or her) disdain for the machine, the craftsman had no role to play in reform (Mairet 1939: 22).

Mairet's ideas are in fact closer to those of Morris than she might have liked to admit, for among craftworkers in Britain in the first half of the twentieth century, Morris was the not-always-popular measure of comparison. Morris was much more interested in fabrics that incorporated pattern into the weave, requiring much larger looms and experienced workers than the geometric form of weaving preferred by Mairet. However, both shared the love of quality raw materials, natural dyes, hand processing, and fair wages. Though Morris was much more concerned with the Medieval and Gothic style, his concern with standards of production and conditions of manufacture were a legacy continued by Mairet (Parry 1983: 7–9, 58).

It is into this legacy that Mairet's attempt to balance profit-making, socialist ideas, handweaving, industry, and natural and synthetic wools falls. Her interest in the machine aesthetic came about through a collaboration with the Swiss-born weaver (and her friend and correspondent) Marianne Straub, whose work in industrial design, training at the Brantford Technical College, understanding of the technical aspects of weaving and experimental approach to materials and weaving were of great importance to Mairet. Traveling together to Europe, the two investigated the modern weaving industry on the continent, which was, to both of their thinking much more advanced in the use of hand-designs for machine production than the British industry (Coatts 1983: 98). Perhaps here, as in the Indian/British hybrid fabrics, Mairet's politics and weaving merge to produce a series of textiles into which are written her attempts to bring together machine and (wo)man through the combination of synthetic and natural wools in hand-designed fabrics, whose patterns would then be passed on to industrial weavers. Not a concession on her part, but rather an attempt to maintain a utopian mastery over the machine, the resulting materials are at once potentially socialist and capitalist—reflecting her own ambiguous position toward a commodity aesthetic.

In the late 1920s, Ethel's marriage to Philip Mairet broke up as he left her for a younger woman (Coatts 1983: 85). From this time, Mairet is referred to as "impatient" and "intolerant." Peter Collingwood offers a description, describing the numerous weavers and interested parties who visited The Gospels: "I sensed the respect they felt for Mrs. Mairet—even when her criticism reduced them to tears… She spoke little (and found me 'the most boring person I have ever met' as she announced over one frugal supper) but she conveyed great authority and somehow I began to accept her judgment over what was a good color, a good yarn, a good feel to a textile" (Collingwood 1983: 22). Collingwood's first-hand account is set against that of Alan Crawford who suggests that "[h]er work was the only thing Ethel Mairet had to hold onto," offering a hyperbolic suggestion that without it she would surely have descended into the vortex of hysteria and misery started by her divorce from Coomaraswamy (Crawford 1984: 46). But this was also the time that The Gospels was prospering, and as Philip Mairet found himself moving away, Lynda Nead's comments might be helpful by way of explanation. Nead writes: "Working women transgressed bourgeois definitions of respectability and female dependency; their imagined sexuality and economic autonomy made them objects of threat" (Nead 1988: 31). Certainly Mairet's own writing does not echo

Crawford's comment that she "did not live a very happy life" (Crawford 1984: 46). Instead, she interprets it quite differently, writing "I thank God for my very varied and beautiful life—full of wonderful experiences of ups and downs."[23] While this is not to suggest that Mairet was not also constructing herself in her writing, the gap between accounts is illuminating.

In spite of emotional upheaval, Mairet continued to maintain a number of close friendships, and ran The Gospels as a successful business. Its proximity to London allowed it to become a gathering place for would-be weavers, though unlike the Arts and Crafts Guild of Handicraft, which was run democratically, The Gospels was run as an apprenticeship program, with Mairet firmly in charge (Coatts 1983: 94–6). This was, however, no cult of personality, as all goods left not with Mairet's name on them, but with the name of the collective. In a sense this went against the policy of many arts and crafts practitioners, who felt that each member working on any given design should be given credit, but Mairet had a specific purpose in mind by doing this. During the period, Mairet, like a number of other designers in Britain, was benefiting from government interest in supporting the arts, which often translated into a wish to structure the discipline of design as a profession, along the lines of law or architecture. Recognized training, registration and regulation, professional associations, links to official government bodies, public recognition, and, in this case the ability to distinguish between designers, were all important in highlighting the difference between amateur and professional production (Seddon 2000: 427–8).

Because the weavings done by The Gospels were considered first the work of women weavers rather than artists, and second were considered to be outside of the art canon, keeping the name as the Gospels allowed for a certain notoriety to build up. Further, because as Jill Seddon points out, women were generally only included on government committees as representatives of the housewife and consumer (Seddon 2000: 429),[24] highlighting the gender-neutral name of The Gospels can be seen as an attempt to make a name for the collective that would elevate handweaving to the status of art. As such, Mairet subscribed wholeheartedly to the Ruskinian notion of the artist as transcendental genius, arguing clearly that the weaver was also an artist. She wrote in her 1942 book on handweaving and education that:

An artist, in whatever branch of art or craft, is a visionary. He looks forward as well as backwards; but forward looking is stronger than backward looking. He sees and feels the future a little more acutely than the ordinary man in the street… By the crowd he is generally called selfish, self-centered, over-riding people and things, believing in himself too much, conceited. He does unbelievable things, things that cannot be generally accepted by the average person. (Mairet 1942: 7)

One wonders if she is talking about herself. Rather than getting rid of the notion of genius (the tactic suggested by many feminist scholars in the 1970s and 1980s), Mairet sought to place weaving into the patriarchal canon. In her thinking, weaving deserved recognition as an art, and its practitioners, whether male or female, recognition as "genius" artists.[25]

Following this line of thinking, Mairet desperately wanted weaving to become part of the school curriculum. Mairet's project, which she actually termed the "formation of taste," was a thinly-disguised plea not only to have weaving accepted as an occupation for boys and girls, but was also a backdoor attempt to gain recognition for her art. Art, for Mairet, was much more than a hobby, and she wrote:

[it needs to be] thought of as an essential part of everything we do; it is as essential in the building of a bridge or a house as the basic work of an engineer or the architect; it cannot be considered a thing apart; it is the unconscious expression of all work. (Mairet 1929: 49)

In her writing, Mairet rarely, if ever, mentions gender as a defining principle in her work or life. It is thus that which is left unsaid that comes through in her incorporation of masculine aspects of machine weaving into her work, and in her definition of the weaver as genius artist—it is the unconscious expression of all of her work. By selling her weavings at a cost that allowed her to make a living, Mairet moved beyond domestic practice, creating a feminine-masculine hybrid textile, but also moving into a relation with capitalism at odds with her socially-conscious outlook. In spite of this, her view of herself differs significantly from that constructed for her by later authors. She came to define herself as "the brain of the machine" (Mairet 1929: 15) noting that: "weaving is not just a pretty pastime but a serious job. The weaving workshops are in fact research laboratories for industry."[26]

Thus we have come full circle—even as Mairet defines herself as "the brain" behind the machinery, her agency is effectively removed through accounts that highlight her intuition in a throwback to discourse from the 1920s and 30s that defined design as a suitable field for women to enter because of its links to ideas of beauty, decorativeness and domesticity (Seddon 2000: 431). The effacement of Ethel Mairet is not a violent one, she is not torn from history, written-over, or viciously erased, but merely forgotten, overlooked or, most importantly, misinterpreted. Her influence still resonates in British design, yet her life presents such a complicated tangling and raveling of gender and ethnic roles that she remains largely unstudied.

Looking back on her life, Mairet wrote to her former husband Ananda Coomaraswamy:

For a time our lives developed very much on the same lines then, quite ... you went on one way and I on another. But I feel very certain that if we had not had those years together we should neither of us have been such distinguished people. And if we had stuck together we should probably have hurt each other very badly. Just as [Philip Mairet] and I agreed to stick to each other for ten years and then we let the time go by, which was a mistake... But you never deceived me and [Philip Mairet] did. That I find exceedingly difficult to understand even now. I have come to the conclusion it is something in myself that is wrong. I am good up to a certain point and then I just go off the deep end. I did with you and I see now that I behaved abominably after a very lovely life with you. I could have been much nicer and more reasonable—more womanly perhaps and more forgiving and understanding. That is all past. I don't regret any part of my life. It is part of my make up. And we both have had a better life because of it. I love work and I love risk. Ever since I left you I have crept along, always in debt, always on the edge of disaster but never quite—always overdrawn, always borrowing. But it has been worthwhile. (Mairet 1945)[27]

Her brief words summarize a life with ups and downs, but one that Mairet herself looked back on as a success. Peter Collingwood concludes his review of his former teacher's exhibition with the words: "This was the message she was always trying to hammer home; that handweaving dealt with the present, that it should be concerned with new materials, be in touch with the newest movements in art and architecture; and that, above all, it was certainly not a delightful and folksy wander down memory lane" (Collingwood 1983: 22). It is a fitting tribute, and one that captures Mairet's ideology, as well as some of her acidity.

To bring all of these threads together, one might look at the practice of handweaving today in Sri Lanka, where traditional craft is often practiced only as participatory development projects, rather than as a part of the daily life envisioned by Coomaraswamy, Gandhi and Mairet. In these projects, usually funded by Western NGOs, women are employed in order to revive traditional crafts through co-operative structures. Although Kamala Peiris, director of one such project, claims that the handweavers working in her village have a better standard of living than many women in Sri Lanka, the colonialist tropes present in Mairet's day are still apparent in many of these projects (Peiris 1997: 1). In Peiris's writing, it is obvious that the traditional practice of male weavers outlined in *Medieval Sinhalese Art*, has become a female practice in line with western norms, while the project is supported by an imperialist imperative that advocates moral lessons such as the importance of saving money and gaining self-reliance, along with the teaching of craft (Peiris 1997: 30).

Furthermore, present day weaving in Sri Lanka might be more readily associated with massive transnational corporate trade—Sri Lanka is home to a number of sweatshops, making clothing and fabric for the Western world (see e.g. Collins 2003). It seems a perverse upheaval of the Coomaraswamy's utopianism with regard to Sinhalese weaving, and an unfortunate legacy into which Mairet's own brand of seemingly innocuous imperialism can be located. The manufacturing that she was so intent on combining with handweaving has been largely removed from Britain and Western Europe, leaving in its wake an ideological vacuum for the crafts, setting them up as luxurious commodities set against cheaply manufactured goods from the East. Mairet's project, her combination of handweaving and modern life, her blurring and crossing of boundaries, seem part of a past that is far from the globalized present. The reclamation of her varied life, and of her utopian spirit might be thus that much more important.

Acknowledgments

I would like to thank Dr. Janice Helland (Queen's University), the McGill Centre for Research and Teaching on Women, and Jean Vacher at the Crafts Study Centre in Farnham for their help with this paper. I would also like to thank craft historian Margot Coatts for publishing her monograph on Ethel Mairet, a detailed biography that provided the base from which this analysis could take place.

Notes

1. Ethel Mairet was born Ethel Partridge. She took the name Ethel Coomaraswamy after her first marriage, and changed it to Ethelmary Coomaraswamy after her first divorce. She then became Ethelmary (or Ethel) Mairet after her second marriage, a name she kept after her second divorce. For the sake of simplicity, I have referred to her as Ethel Mairet throughout. The only comprehensive account of Mairet's life is Margot Coatts's *A Weaver's Life: Ethel Mairet, 1872–1952* (1983). This work is a labor of love as Coatts has done a remarkable job in recapturing and uncovering the details of a life that would otherwise have been completely lost. Without Coatts's catalogue this essay would have been impossible.
2. In her lifetime, Mairet was well enough known to be given an exhibition at the Metropolitan Museum in New York in 1942 (Waller 1984: 78).
3. Lethaby edited the *Artistic Crafts Series of Technical Handbooks*, a series of books that preached a John Ruskin-style anti-industrialism. His book on handlooms, however, might have influenced Mairet, for it forcefully argued that weaving should be designed as part of its process, rather than separately (Harrod 1999: 18).
4. Coomaraswamy was born in Sri Lanka to a Sri Lankan father and a British mother. He was educated in Britain, but returned periodically to Sri Lanka before finally settling in the USA, where he became an art historian at the Boston Museum of Fine Arts, publishing more than 900 articles before his death in 1947. Though important during his lifetime,

his importance today to post-colonial and (perhaps surprisingly) anarchist scholars is enormous, and not to be underestimated (see Lipsey 1977).

5. The full quote reads: "Colour and yarn were what she loved. Her instincts were simple and attached themselves to the materials of weaving, what is there at the start; pattern and structure mattered less and were, in a sense, beyond her; she 'designed' her textiles by making decisions at the loom" (Crawford 1984: 46).

6. Coomaraswamy wrote in the introduction: "This book is not primarily intended as a work of scholarship, but is written first of all for the Sinhalese people, as a memorial of a period which at present they are not willing to understand. The 'educated' Sinhalese of to-day, after, on the one hand, a century of foreign government, and of education in which the national culture has been completely ignored, and, on the other hand, an equal period of subservience and obsequious imitation of foreign manners, have little reason to be proud of their present achievement in the Art of Living. Evidence of shallow thought is everywhere to be seen in an exaltation of the present age at the expense of the past." He continues that it is meant as a contribution to understanding the past, but also for those in the East and West "interested in the reorganization of life, and especially of the arts and crafts until modern conditions," before remarking that the Sinhalese people need to look to their past, rather than the degraded and colonized present for inspiration (Coomaraswamy 1956: vi).

7. Mairet wrote to C. R. Ashbee "The coloring and dresses are so wonderful – men as well as women. The men nearly always in fine white muslin, trousers – but trousers which *fit* and which are beautiful (I never knew trousers could be beautiful before!) and a long coat embroidered with fine white embroidery, always spotlessly clean. There is a sense of culture which I have never felt anywhere so keenly. You feel you are among people who know what real civilization means" (quoted in Singham 1974: 41).

8. The sources are too numerous to list here, but the work of the Subaltern Studies Collective, for example, founded in 1982 has promoted the study of formerly colonized countries, resulting in an entire area of postcolonial studies.

9. In part the use of synthetic materials might have been born of necessity. During the Second World War, wool was rationed, but cellophane and other materials were not (Schoeser 1997: 86).

10. Letter to Marianne Straub, December 1937, Envelope 33, Ethel Mairet Archive.

11. Letter to Ananda Coomaraswamy, May 1941, Envelope 40, Ethel Mairet Archive.

12. Letter to Marianne Straub, February 2, 1940, Envelope 33,

Ethel Mairet Archive. Most of Mairet's students were middle class ladies "gentlewomen under no particular pressure to earn a living" (quoted in Harrod 1999: 152). There must have been, in a sense, a constant tension between Mairet's financial state of permanent debt and the attitude of her middle class students that boils up in this letter about the unfortunate Olive.
13. Letter to Marianne Straub, Jan 18, 1941, Envelope 33, Ethel Mairet Archive.
14. Letter to Marianne Straub, undated, 1941, Envelope 33, Ethel Mairet Archive.
15. Ethel Mairet Archive.
16. Alice Richardson, who eloped with Coomaraswamy had been friends with Philip Mairet at the Hornsey School of Art. She had also been good friends with the textile artists Phyllis Barron and Dorothy Larcher (Harrod 1999: 50).
17. In 1836 two marriage acts: An Act for Marriage in England and An Act for Registering Births, Deaths and Marriages created a central Registry Office and registrars through the country who could carry out civil marriages. As Lynda Nead notes, "compulsory registration emphasized licit and illicit sexual behavior and allowed for a greater regulation of extra-marital sex" (Nead 1988: 35). In his autobiography, Philip Mairet also noted that before Ethel's divorce went through, the two had to be very careful about not being caught in their relationship, primarily for the sake of morality, but also because of the divorce proceedings (Sisson; pp. 55–68). In the end, the novelty of the marriage contract proved too great, and the Mairets registered their marriage.
18. At the time Ditchling was an artists' community—not only Mairet, but also calligrapher Edward Johnson, letter-cutter and sculptor Eric Gill, and others lived there (Harrod 1999: 29).
19. The relations between the Partridge family and May Hart's family were not good. Fred Partridge was an unfeeling husband, and May Hart was often consumed with jealousy. After her death, Ethel Mairet adopted their daughter Joan. May Hart Partridge is herself an interesting figure to the study of female craft practitioners, as she herself is at risk of being erased from written histories. In 1969, Joan Partridge wrote to Marianne Straub with regard to her parents' estate "I also have ... one or two of my mother's enamels, which you can also have *if* you take some notice of my mother who I believe [sic] was as good as Dad. No one has ever taken notice of her, I suppose because her death was so untaimely [sic] and such a family skeliton [sic], but I think it would be frightful if her work did not live." Joan's effort to save her mother's work is heightened through her separation from her family. Her mother, she writes "was a forbidden subject of enquiry," while her mother's sister felt that she "was part of my mother's great mistake [of marrying Fred Partridge] and she didn't half make me realize that." (Letter from Joan Partridge to Marianne Straub, March 3 1969, Ethel Mairet Archives).
20. Envelope 6, Ethel Mairet Archive.
21. Envelope 6, Ethel Mairet Archive.
22. Letter to Marianne Straub, 18 January 1941. Envelope 33, Ethel Mairet Archive.
23. Letter to Ananda Coomaraswamy, May 8, 1941. Ethel Mairet Archive.
24. It should be noted, however, that the Faculty of Royal Designers for Industry, in existence from 1936 to 1951, elected forty-three men and RDIs, and four women, including Ethel Mairet (Seddon 2000: 437).
25. In this, Mairet was somewhat radical. Because she was a self-taught weaver, and had not learned textile arts in the traditional manner of a mother to daughter legacy, she was already outside of the domestic learning that might have more closely bonded her work to the domestic, rather than public space.
26. *Sussex Daily News*, June 10, 1940, Envelope 6, Ethel Mairet Archive.
27. Letter to Ananda Coomaraswamy, May 8, 1945, Envelope 40, Ethel Mairet Collection Archive. Coomaraswamy replied to this letter "I was touched by your

personal words. I do not think you have anything to reproach yourself for, rather, I was impossibly difficult and you were very patient. On the other hand, of course, by the time we reach our age, one looks back and seems to see that the course of one's life had some direction…" (June 1, 1945, Envelope 40).

References

Advisory Committee. 1946. "Woven textiles." *The Architectural Review* 99 (March): 91–92.

Bachmann, Ingrid and Ruth Scheuing (eds). 1998. *Material Matters: The Art and Culture of Contemporary Textiles*. Toronto: YYZ Book.

Bean, Susan S. 1989. "Gandhi and *Khadi*, the fabric of Indian independence." In Jane Schneider and Annette B. Weiner (eds). *Cloth and the Human Experience*. Washington and London: Smithsonian Institution Press; pp. 355–76.

Bhabha, Homi. 1994. *The Location of Culture*. New York and London: Routledge.

Brantlinger, Patrick. 1996. "A postindustrial prelude to postcolonialism: John Ruskin, William Morris, and Gandhism." *Critical Inquiry* 22: 466–85.

Buckley, Cheryl. 1989. "Made in patriarchy: toward a feminist analysis of women and design." In Victor Margolin (ed.) 1989. *Design Discourse: History, Theory, Criticism*. Chicago and London: University of Chicago Press; pp. 251–264.

Butler, Judith. 1991. "Imitation and gender insubordination." In Diana Fuss (ed.) 1991. *Inside/Out: Lesbian Theories, Gay Theories*. New York and London: Routledge; pp. 13–31.

Coatts, Margot (ed.) 1983. *Pioneers of Modern Craft*. Manchester and New York: Manchester University Press.

——. 1997. *A Weaver's Life: Ethel Mairet 1872–1952*. Bath: Crafts Council in Association with the Crafts Study Centre.

Collingwood, Peter. 1983. "Gospel of Weaving." *Craft (London)* 64 (Sep/Oct): 22–25.

Collins, Jane. 2003. *Threads: Gender, Labor and Power in the Global Apparel Industry*. Chicago and London: University of Chicago Press.

Coomaraswamy, Ananda. 1956. *Medieval Sinhalese Art*, Second Edition. New York: Pantheon Books.

Coomaraswamy, Ethel. 1916. *A Book on Vegetable Dyes*. Hammersmith: Hampshire House Workshops.

Crawford, Alan. 1984. "A weaver's life: review." *Crafts (London)* 68: 46.

Crowley, David. 1995. "The uses of peasant design in Austria-Hungary in the late nineteenth and early twentieth centuries." *Studies in the Decorative Arts* (Spring): 2–28.

Deepwell, Katy (ed.) 1995. *New Feminist Art Criticism*. Manchester and New York: Manchester University Press.

Defries, Amelia. 1924. "Craftsmen of the empire: a comparative study of decoration and industrial arts." *The Architecture Review* IV (June): 261–71.

Ethel Mairet Files, Craft Study Centre, Farnham, Surrey, England.

Greenhalgh, Paul. 2000. "Le style anglais: English roots of the new art." In Paul Greenhalgh (ed.) 2000. *Art Nouveau 1890–1914*. London: V&A Publications; pp. 126–47.

Harrod, Tanya. 1996. "Ananda Coomaraswamy: his ideas and influence." *Crafts (London)* 143 (November/December): 20–23.

——. 1999. *The Crafts in Britain in the Twentieth Century*. New Haven: Yale University Press and the Bard Graduate Centre for Studies in the Decorative Arts.

Hunt, Anthony. 1937. *Textile Design*. London: The Studio "How to Do It Series."

James, S. 1987. "A weaver's life: Ethel Mairet 1872–1952, Review." *Woman's Art Journal* 8 (Fall–Winter): 59–60.

Krauss, R. 1986. *The Originality of the Avant Garde and Other Modernist Myths*. Cambridge, MA: MIT Press; p. 196.

Lipsey, Roger. 1977. *Coomaraswamy, vol. III, His Life and Work*. Princeton: Bollingen Series 89, Princeton University Press.

Low, Florence B. 1932. "Mrs. Mairet's weaving industry, Ditchling, Sussex." *The Queen*, May 11: 35

Maharaj, Sarat. 1998. "Arachne's genre: towards inter-cultural studies in textiles." In Ingrid Bachmann and Ruth Scheuing (eds.). *Material Matters: The Art and Culture of Contemporary Textiles*. Toronto: YYZ Books; pp. 157–96.

Mairet, Ethel. 1920. *A Book on Vegetable Dyes*. Ditchling, Sussex: St. Dominic's Press.

——. 1929. *Hand-Weaving Notes for Teachers*. London: Faber and Faber.

——. 1939. *Hand-Weaving To-day*. London: Faber and Faber.

——. 1942. *Hand Weaving and Education*. London: Faber and Faber.

Margolin, Victor (ed.). 1989. *Design Discourse: History, Theory, Criticism*. Chicago and London: University of Chicago Press.

Moore, Henrietta. 1994. *A Passion for Difference: Essays in Anthropology and Gender*. Bloomington: Indiana University Press.

Nead, Lynda. 1988. *Myths of Sexuality: Representations of Women in Victorian Britain*. Oxford: Basil Blackwell.

"Obituary: Ethel Mairet." *London Times*, November 26, 1952.

Parker, Rozsika. 1989. *The Subversive Stitch: Embroidery and the Making of the Feminine*. New York: Routledge.

—— and Griselda Pollock. 1981. *Old Mistresses: Women, Art and Ideology*. New York: Pantheon Books.

Parry, Linda. 2000. "The New Textiles." In Paul Greenhalgh (ed.). *Art Nouveau 1890–1914*. London: V&A Publications; pp. 179–191.

——. 1983. *William Morris Textiles*. New York: Viking Press.

Peiris, Kamala. 1997. *Weaving a Future Together: Women and Participatory Development in Sri Lanka*. International Books.

Perron, Mireille. 1998. "Common threads: local strategies for 'inappropriated' artists." In Ingrid Bachmann and Ruth Scheuing (eds.). *Material Matters: The Art and Culture of Contemporary Textiles*. Toronto: YYZ Books; pp. 121–132.

Roscoe, Barley. 1983–84. "Ethel Mairet 1872–1952: A Weaver's Life, Review." *The Studio International* 196/1004: pp. 36–38.

Schneider, Jane and Annette B. Weiner (eds). 1989. *Cloth and the Human Experience*. Washington and London: Smithsonian Institution Press.

Schoeser, Mary. 1997. "Marianne Straub." In Margot Coatts (ed.). *Pioneers of Modern Craft*. Manchester and New York: Manchester University Press; pp. 83–94.

Seddon, Jill. 2000. "Mentioned, but denied significance: women designers and the 'professionalisation of design in Britain c. 1920–1951." *Gender and History* 12/2 (July): 426–47.

Singham, S. D. R. 1974. *Ananda Coomaraswamy: Remembering and Remembering Again and Again*. Kuala Lumpur: Khee Meng Press.

Sisson, C. H. (ed.). 1981. *Autobiographical and Other Papers by Philip Mairet*. Manchester: Carcanet.

Waller, Irene. 1984. "A weaver's life, Ethel Mairet, 1872–1952: Review." *Fiberart* 11 (July/Aug): 78–79.

Exhibition Review
The *arttextiles* Project: An Ongoing Concern

Exhibition Review
The *arttextiles* Project: An Ongoing Concern

A touring exhibition organized by Bury St Edmunds Art Gallery 2004–6

In September 2004, *arttextiles3* opened at the Bury St Edmunds Art Gallery in England, the third in a series of major surveys of work by British artists engaging with textiles. The exhibition project began with *arttextiles1* in 1996 and has continued on a four-year cycle with *arttextiles2* being held in 2000. The project is made available to audiences through an extended UK-wide tour, and a major publication that forms an excellent catalogue to *arttextiles3* and also provides an invaluable summary of, and opportunity for critical reflection on the twelve-year project. A discussion website also plays a role.

The Project

The guiding hand behind all three exhibitions has been the former director of Bury St Edmunds, Barbara Taylor. A review of the whole project seems timely, because the comprehensive publication which accompanies *arttextiles3* offers the reader an insight into the concept which shaped the development of all three shows. It also seems timely because, in early 2005, Barbara Taylor left her directorship of the Bury St Edmunds Art Gallery to pursue a freelance career. Therefore, the future of the project itself appears to be at a crossroads.

During a conversation with Barbara Taylor (December 2004), she informed this reviewer that, when she joined the gallery in 1993, one of her preoccupations was the lack of sustained exhibition opportunity for art textiles in Britain in comparison with both Europe and the USA. The gallery's then-education officer, Irene Edwards, had promoted a related idea, which Taylor eventually developed as the *arttextiles* project; this sought to establish a distinctive role for the gallery regionally, nationally and internationally in terms of contemporary visual culture, while still serving a traditional conservative local audience.

Throughout the project's development Barbara Taylor saw her role as project director. Each *arttextiles* survey show was created through a process of open

REVIEWED BY POLLY BINNS

submission and selection; in putting together the three selection panels, Taylor was aware that her choice would inevitably shape the nature of each exhibition, and that it would direct the shift in debate that occurred around each survey. One selector was "carried forward" between each show to ensure continuity; I undertook this role between *arttextiles1* and *2* and Sarat Maharaj between *2* and *3*. For *arttextiles1* the selection panel[1] was composed of practitioners representing a very broad approach to working in textiles; all were significantly engaged in Higher Level Education in Britain at that stage of the 1990s and were aware of what was up and coming from undergraduate programs. In addition, a conscious choice was made to include expertise in the area of tapestry. The application form addressed the invitation to submit to "textile artists." From the vantage point of the present, Taylor's criticism of that process was that it had been too internal and subject to personal politics.

The second survey show, which toured during 2000–2, was selected by a group of individuals diversely engaged with practise and critical theory.[2] The selectors' interests encouraged and focused on external critiques and the resulting exhibition marked a discernible shift towards intellectual and conceptual engagements rather than practise through material. Taylor's view was that, in the early 1990s, art textiles had seemed to require special pleading for a role and location within the contemporary visual arts and that the practise thus suffered from over-cocooning.

The ambition now, she argued, was for the work selected to challenge that position, to start questioning what was so important about the use of textiles in fine-art practise. The second survey, therefore, invited submissions from "artists working with textiles" and succeeded in challenging boundaries and mindsets. The diversity of interests of the artists who applied for *arttextiles2* was testimony to how wide engagement was within contemporary practise. The ambition for submissions to *arttextiles3*[3] was to expand further the understanding of the practise and one of its primary objectives was to examine whether there could, in fact, still be seen to be a practise identifiable as art textiles. The invitation was to artists "who reference textiles."

The Exhibition

An immediate issue raised by *arttextiles3* is the question of curatorial decision-making and exhibitions created by open submission. At first glance, the range of work is of variable confidence and quality; the selectors were not relying on the "established" and "the best" from within a familiar framework. The choice of selectors certainly influenced submissions from some of the most interesting artists exhibiting, and whose current work, I would argue, would not have come to light other than through this system of open invitation. The selection for *arttextiles3* brought together for debate the work of about 450 artists. The discussions that took place over the period of selection could not have occurred within a critical framework established by a curator initiating such an exhibition. The selection process stimulated debates, and suggested fresh connections and different trains of thought around the work that the selectors viewed, which impacted on their response to it at that time.

The resulting exhibition is very much the product of those lines of enquiry that emerged from the selection process. The inclusion of work by one artist in particular—Tony Rickaby's *Canvas Factory—Work Song* (2004)—should be seen as a direct result of this selection process (Figure 1). Rickaby is a well-established artist; for him to participate in this open submission proposes a new association for his work, a sense of "seizing" the moment in a developmental stage. This one piece of work, Taylor argues, represents a justification for the selection policy. It enables thinking about textiles to grow, and places it in the serious debating arena. In addition, the selection has thrown light on how the exhibition is installed and developed in the gallery space. Access to the debates around the selection process allows new associations to be made and relationships to be perceived by the viewer in the juxtaposition of works.

The siting of work selected for *arttextiles3* has moved beyond the gallery space in Gerard Williams's work, *Interior Worlds* (2004) (Figures 2 and 3). Standing in the gallery at Bury St Edmunds, the viewer was invited to look out of the window across the street to what, at a first, casual glance, appeared to be the frontage of a building of mixed occupancy, with commercial tenants on the street frontage at ground-floor level to domestic spaces on the upper floors. A telescope positioned at the gallery window invited the usually illicit activity of "peeping" in at these windows. A moment or two's reflection, however, revealed the intention behind the work, as one gradually understood that each window was dressed, and had been given a prescribed identity. An imaginary family was created and a narrative implied, allowing our imaginations to travel their own individual journeys. One derived a further, slightly guilty pleasure from overhearing the exclamations of other visitors as they succumbed to peering through the telescope, and made their own discoveries. Their imaginings fueled one's own.

Gerard Williams's work also invites reflection on how installation may be captured for an extended audience. The catalogue

Figure 1
Tony Rickaby, *Canvas Factory—Work Song* (2004).

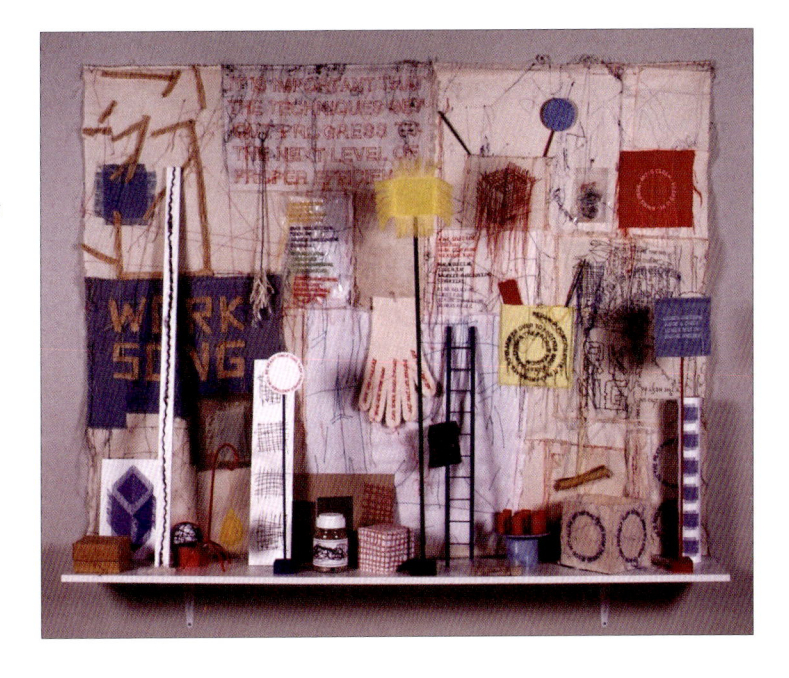

Figure 2
Gerard Williams, *Interior Worlds* (2004). Proposal for Bury St Edmunds installation.

Figure 3
Gerard Williams, *Interior Worlds* (2004). View of the block across the street from Bury St Edmunds Art Gallery.

section of the publication includes an image of the artist's impression of the installation, which is how it was experienced by the audience at Bury St Edmunds. The first venue of the tour in Edinburgh allowed a new installation; further venues cannot guarantee such an opportunity. However, the website is a repository of images taken by the artist of each installation site and will allow the work to be "followed" as the tour progresses. The work may also be seen as bringing together, in a sense, the *arttextiles* project with its sister *Textiles on Site* project, and acknowledges within the exhibition artwork which is out of context in the gallery space.

The Publication

Access to the debates that took place around the selection is facilitated through the publication accompanying *arttextiles3*. As part of its development and while the work selected was in the gallery, a seminar was held to allow an invited audience to engage with the panel, and extensive notes on the ensuing discussion are included in the publication. At the seminar, Barbara Taylor invited the audience to submit essays to further the debate in the publication. Pamela Johnson and Victoria Mitchell publish eminently thoughtful essays on current locations for art textiles, while essays by the other contributors debate the work of specific artists in the exhibition.

The publication also includes summaries of both the previous surveys together with images of all the work, which allows anyone the opportunity for new reflections on the *Textiles on Site* project, an associated initiative that has been run in conjunction with each survey exhibition. This partnership project was designed by Bury St Edmunds Art Gallery to create commissions for artists using textile to make site-specific works for public spaces both in buildings and outside, and intended to run alongside each exhibition in the gallery. One ambition was to bring on board other local authorities and to provide opportunities for the artists selected to work with clients from outside the arts world. It also created an exhibiting framework for artists whose work does not, perhaps, always use the gallery space as a context. It is interesting, in this respect, to consider Caroline Bartlett's work in *arttextiles1—Threshold* (1996)—alongside her major installation *Codices*, an ephemeral piece of land art sited in the Abbey Gardens throughout the summer of 2000 (Figures 4 and 5). The two works demonstrate succinctly the personal development of an artist's work. The ongoing relationship

Figure 4
Caroline Bartlett, *Threshold* (1996). Cotton and silk triptych using discharge and direct printing and pleating.

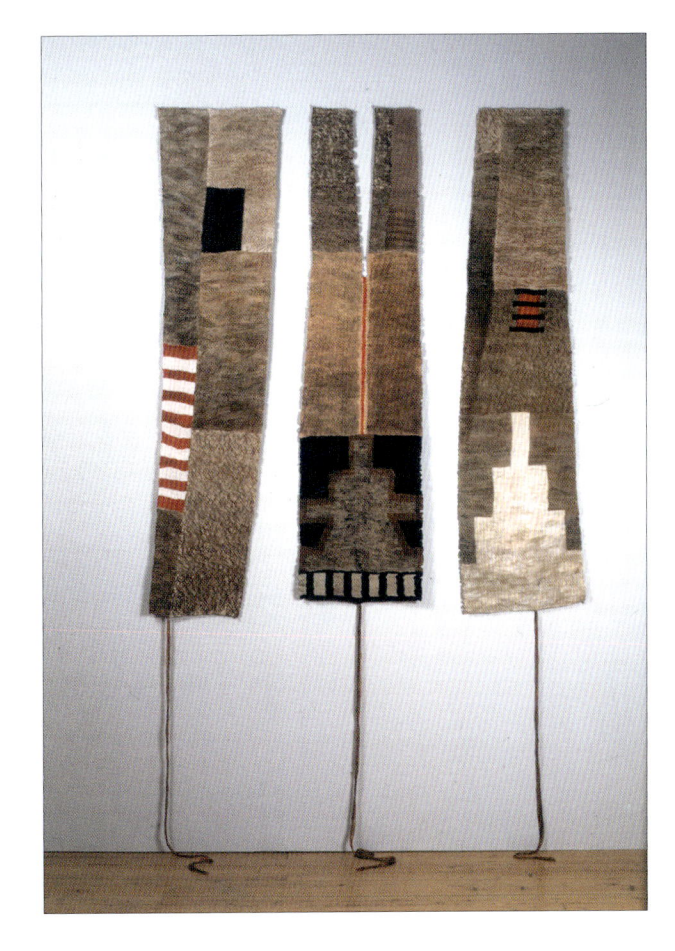

developed through this initiative with the Abbey Gardens and the Cathedral has been a notable success of the project and has created a real relevance for both permanent and ephemeral textile art in Bury. This is a singular achievement in itself for the gallery.

Several of the works in the exhibition are time based and a further initiative of the publication is to include a DVD of these digital works containing short, edited excerpts from each artist. The DVD serves as an excellent *aide-memoir* for those who have visited and experienced the works in their entirety installed as each artist intended, whether on monitors or projected. How successful it is in allowing the "reader" of the catalogue to engage with the work is debatable, but it remains nonetheless an interesting development and a great improvement on the ubiquitous video-still image of the standard catalogue.

Project Constants

The quality of the catalogues has been a consistent strength with each survey exhibition. The original print run of 4,000 copies for *arttextiles1* was exhausted several years ago; to date, I understand over 3,000 copies of *arttextiles2* have been sold. Each publication has become requisite reading for textile students on degree level courses in the UK, as they offer a unique encapsulation of the debates around art textiles/textile art over the last decade or so and have done much to support the ensuing and expanding debates around the subject. The *Textiles on Site* partner project has also created a dynamic within the city and given artists using textile creative opportunities to explore the production of work in situ on a scale seldom to be found in Britain.

Each of the survey shows has enjoyed extended tours; by the end of the *arttextiles3* program, the exhibitions will have visited

Figure 5
Caroline Bartlett, working on *Codices* for the Abbey Gardens, 2000.

twenty-one venues throughout the UK. Perhaps the most telling evidence of the interest there is for the subject in the UK has been the numbers of visitors calculated to have seen the shows over the twelve-year lifespan of the project. Estimated attendances have reached 75,000; the Harley Gallery in Nottinghamshire alone received 11,000 visitors through its doors for *arttextiles2* and is included again in the current tour. Since the project's inception, Taylor's philosophy has been that what is developed, as a product, is what is significant. It is not important if there is not a ready-made audience geographically in the immediate locale of the initiating venue. Far more people have seen the exhibitions on tour than has ever been the case at Bury.

The original ambition for *arttextiles1* was to develop a project that explored and helped to sustain the expanded field of art textiles/textile art. *arttextiles3*, in relation to both the work in the exhibition and the publication, demonstrates that there is still ground to cover and further territories to explore. The future of the project is at a crossroads and itself the subject of debate as Barbara Taylor steps aside. As a sustained and rigorous inquiry into the subject area it is the only project of its kind within the UK. It has established a significant history for itself and has the authority to carry the debates forward into the future.

All the details of the *arttextiles* project may be found on the website www.arttextiles.org The site also includes a discussion board. All enquiries about the project should be addressed to enquiries@burystedmundsartgallery.org.

Notes
1. Selectors: Polly Binns, Michael Brennand-Wood, Lisa Collins
2. Selectors: Dr Polly Binns, Professor Sarat Maharaj, Yinka Shonibare, Gill Hedley
3. Selectors: Susan Hiller, Professor Sarat Maharaj, Sarah Quinton, Jonathon Watkins

ARLIS/UK & Ireland Annual Conference
University of Northumbria at Newcastle upon Tyne, UK
Wednesday 19th – Friday 21st July 2006

ARLIS UK & Ireland Art Libraries Society

'The Baltic and Beyond'

Join us for next year's conference at Northumbria University's vibrant city centre campus. Newcastle, once at the leading edge of 19th Century industrial innovation, is now in the forefront of technical innovation, leisure and culture. The city's quayside is recently transformed, including the Millennium Bridge spanning the River Tyne to the Baltic Centre and Gateshead Quays.

The conference will focus on the 'Baltic and Beyond', with sessions on:
- Building bridges
- Transnational relations
- Industrial past and technical futures

Applications are invited for a single fully-funded place* for a first-time delegate from outside the UK and Ireland to attend the ARLIS/UK & Ireland Annual Conference:

International Delegate Award

The Baltic and Beyond: Newcastle upon Tyne, 19th – 21st July 2006

To apply for the award, please submit the following by email or post by Friday 26th May 2006:
1. A completed application form (see: www.arlis.org.uk or from the address below)
2. A résumé listing educational background, employment history and   professional activities.

The winner must confirm in writing that he/she is able to meet the requirement of conference attendance. The recipient will be expected to submit a post-conference report to the ARLIS/UK & Ireland Council. The decisions of the Council of ARLIS/UK & Ireland and its Grants Panel shall be final, and no correspondence regarding these shall be entered into. The Council of ARLIS/UK & Ireland reserves the right to make no award if no suitable application is received.
*NB The award does not include travel costs

Application papers should be returned to Anna Mellows at the address below.

For further information on the Annual Conference 2006 please check the ARLIS/UK & Ireland website: www.arlis.org.uk

or contact:
Anna Mellows, Administrator, ARLIS/UK & Ireland,
Courtauld Institute of Art, Somerset House, Strand, London, WC2R 0RN,UK
Email: arlis@courtauld.ac.uk, Tel: + 44 (0) 20 7848 2703